THE POETICAL WORKS OF
THOMAS TRAHERNE

An Hymne upon St Bartholomews Day.

1
What powerfull Spirit lives within!
What Active Angel doth inhabit here!
What Heavenly Light inspires my Skin;
Which doth so like a DEITIE appear
A LIVING TEMPLE of all Ages &
Within me see
A TEMPLE OF ETERNITIE!
All Kingdoms I Descrie
In me.

2
An Inward Omnipresence here,
Mysteriously like His within me stands,
Whose Knowledg is a Sacred Sphere
That in it self at once Includes all Lands.
There is som ANGEL y within Me can
Both Talk & Move
And Walk & flie & See & love
A Man on Earth, a Man
Above.

3
Dull Walls of Clay my SPIRIT leavs
And in a forrein Kingdom doth appear,
This Great Apostle it receivs
Admires his WORKS, standing here
Within my Self from East to West I moves,
As if I were
At once a CHERUBIM & Sphere...
Or was at once abov,
And here.

4
The Souls a Messenger wherby
Within... Inward Temples Wewmtg be
Even like thy very Dietie,
In all thy parts of His Eternities.
O liv within & leav unwildy Dross
Flesh is but Clay!
O fly my Soul & Haste away,
To JESUS THRONE, or CROSS
Obey!

Facsimile of the original MS.
of one of Traherne's Poems

THE POETICAL WORKS OF
THOMAS TRAHERNE
1636?–1674

FROM THE ORIGINAL MANUSCRIPTS

EDITED BY
BERTRAM DOBELL

WITH A MEMOIR OF THE AUTHOR

SECOND EDITION

"I give you the end of a golden string,
Only wind it into a ball,
It will lead you in at Heaven's gate
Built in Jerusalem's wall."
William Blake

"Heaven lies about us in our infancy."
William Wordsworth

Angelico Press

For information, address:
Angelico Press, Ltd.
169 Monitor St.
Brooklyn, NY 11222
www.angelicopress.com

Paperback: 979-8-88677-130-5
Cloth: 979-8-88677-131-2

Book and cover design
by Michael Schrauzer

G. THORN DRURY

My youth was ever constant to one dream,
Though hope failed oft—so hopeless did it seem—
That in the ripeness of my days I might
Something achieve that should the world requite
For my existence ; for it was a pain
To think that I should live and live in vain :
And most my thoughts were turned towards the Muse,
Though long she did my earnest prayers refuse,
And left me darkling and despairing ; then
By happy chance there came within my ken
A hapless poet, whom—I thank kind fate !—
It was my privilege to help instate
In that proud eminence wherein he shines
Now that no more on earth he sadly pines.
This was a fortune such as I must ever
Be thankful for—yet still 'twas my endeavour,
With what, I hope, was no unworthy zeal,
My life-work with some other deed to seal,

And lo ! when such a dream might well seem vain,
Propitious fate smiled on me once again,
And through the mists of time's close-woven pall
A glint of light on one dim form did fall,
Which, as I gazed more earnestly, became
A living soul, discovered by the flame
Of glowing inspiration which possessed
Even now, as when he lived, the poet's breast.
Did I deceive myself ?   Could it be true
A new poetic star was in my view,
And shining with a lustre bright and clear,
Where, constellated in the heavenly sphere,
Herbert and Vaughan, Crashaw and Milton shine
With varying brightness, yet alike divine ?
I gazed again, but still that star burned on,
And ever with a deeper radiance shone,
Until I knew no Will-o'-th'-Wisp's false light,
No meteor delusive mocked my sight,
But 'twas indeed a fulgent planet which
Henceforth shall with its beams the heavens enrich.

Some vanity, I know, is in this strain,
But men may be with reason sometimes vain :
Shall he alone who does a worthy deed
Not pay himself, if so he will, that meed
Of self-applause from which all virtues spring,—
Without it who would do a noble thing ?

So let the world arraign me as it will,
It cannot now my satisfaction chill,
Since you, dear friend ! and all whose praise I prize,
Look on my labours with approving eyes.

This book to you 'tis fit I dedicate
Since you, my friend, so well appreciate—
Nay, rather love, our poets of old time,
Responding ever to their notes sublime :
Who, though you treasure most those sons of light,
Whose radiance glitters on the brow of night,
Do not despise the faintest twinkling star
That shines where Shakespeare, Spenser, Milton are :
Who can, like Lamb, a brilliant flower descry
Where all seems sterile to the common eye,
Who, like Lamb, too, to no strait bounds confined,
Have room for all fair fancies in your mind,
And, with a taste that never errs, discover
Faults like a censor, beauties like a lover.

Here is another offering for your store,
Though not arrayed in that brown garb of yore
Which, with quaint type and paper stained with age,
Were for the Spirit of our Poet-Sage
A fitter dwelling, more becoming page.
I could not give him these, and so have sought
To match his noble and exalted thought

DEDICATION

With the best raiment that our time affords
Of comely type, fine paper, seemly boards,
Which, centuries hence, to our children's children's eyes
May have an antique look which they shall prize,
When Traherne's name, familiar to their ears,
Shall hold assured a place among his peers.

CONTENTS

CONTENTS

CONTENTS

*_** The poems of which the titles are enclosed within brackets are
without titles in the original manuscripts. It seemed better to
give them names, in order to facilitate reference to them.

INTRODUCTION

It is with a more than ordinary degree of pleasure that I have undertaken the task of introducing to readers of the present day the writings of a hitherto unknown seventeenth-century poet. Centuries had drawn their curtains around him, and he had died utterly, as it seemed, out of the minds and memories of men ; but the long night of his obscurity is at length over, and his light henceforth, if I am not much mistaken, is destined to shine with undiminished lustre as long as England or the English tongue shall endure.

The author of the poems contained in the present volume belongs to that small group of religious poets which includes Herbert, Vaughan, and Crashaw, though he is much more nearly allied to the authors of "The Temple" and "Silex Scintillans" than to the lyrist of Roman Catholicism. Yet he is neither a follower nor an imitator of any of these, but one who draws his inspiration from sources either peculiar to himself or made his own by the moulding force of his own fervent spirit.

Of the inner life of the author of these poems we have abundant and satisfactory knowledge, for it is certain that no man's writings ever furnished a clearer or more faithful mirror of their author's personality than do those of Thomas Traherne. But of the outward incidents of his life little can be told, though that little is sufficient to show that he was a man of the finest and noblest character. Profession and practice in his case went together, and he was no less admirable as a man than he was as a poet and a minister of religion. That he was a person of great sweetness of disposition, of most happy temperament, and of singularly attractive character, is certain ; and to know so much of a man is to know everything we really need to know. We cannot help, however, craving for more than this, and we would give much indeed for such a record of Traherne as Walton gave of Hooker, Herbert, Donne, and Sanderson. It is likely, indeed, that other particulars of Traherne's career will in time be discovered ; but for the present the reader must be content with the scanty details which are given in the following pages.

I regret to say that the inquiries which I have made, or caused to be made, as to the time and place of Thomas Traherne's birth have been, so far, without result. Probably he was born at Hereford, since his father was a shoemaker in that town ; but this is not certain. He may have been born at Ledbury, which is a village a few miles from Hereford, for it seems pretty certain that his family was in some way connected with that place. The earlier portion of the registers of that village has been printed by the Parish Registers Society, and from this it appears that there were "Trayernes" there in the sixteenth century. Unfortunately, the portion of the Ledbury registers which covers the period during which it is probable that our author was born is missing. That also seems to be the case as regards the Hereford registers of the same period. This is very disappointing; but we may hope that further inquiries will prove more successful.

That the family from which the poet sprang was Welsh by descent seems to be highly probable. It is true that the name is also found in a slightly different form in Cornwall; but no doubt both branches sprang from the same root at some distant period. The poet's character and temperament, as displayed in his writings, almost proclaim his nationality. Herbert and Vaughan, the two poets to whom he is most near akin, were both Welsh by descent, and though neither of them is deficient in warmth of feeling, Traherne certainly surpasses them in the passionate fervour which he infuses into his writings. It is hardly possible to think of them as having emanated from the cooler and less enthusiastic Anglo-Saxon temperament.

All that I am able to say, then, as to the time of
Traherne's birth is that it was probably in the year 1636.
Wood informs us that he became a commoner of
Brazennose College, Oxford, in 1652 ; and as the age at
which it was then usual for youths to commence their
college career was about sixteen, the above date seems
the most likely one, though it may, of course, have been
a year earlier or later. His father was in all probability
the "John Traherne, Shoemaker," who is recorded to
have received, in conjunction with another person, "from
Mistress Joyce Jefferies the sum of three pounds for the
shipping money." * This lady is also recorded to have
paid money to one John Traherne (who may or may
not have been the same person) for training as the soldier
whom she had to provide for the Trained-bands.

John Traherne, it seems likely, was related to a man
of considerable note and influence in Hereford. This
was Philip Traherne (the name is sometimes spelt
Traheron), who was twice Mayor of Hereford. He was
born in 1566, and was noted for his fidelity to the cause of
King Charles I., and, to follow the eulogium upon his
tombstone, "for his fervent zeal for the Established
Church and clergy, and friendly and affectionate
behaviour in conversation, which rendered him highly
valuable to all the loyal party." He was mayor of

* See "Archæologia," vol. xxxvii. p. 204.

Hereford at the time when the Scots attacked it. He died in 1645, aged 79. It would thus appear that the Traherne family was one which occupied a fairly good position in the middle class of the community. It would seem, however, from a passage in Traherne's "Centuries of Meditations" ("Sitting in a little obscure room in my father's poor house") that John Traherne's circumstances were not very flourishing.

Of the poet's infancy and youth, the only source of information we have is that which we find in his own writings. That the poems in which he dwells so lovingly, and with so much enthusiasm, upon the happiness and innocence of his infancy are somewhat coloured by the warmth of his imagination may, perhaps, be suspected, but not, I think, with justice. It is possible that he, to some extent, confused reflections of later date with those which he represents himself to have experienced in his infancy ; but he was evidently a very precocious child, and the dawn of consciousness and thought was surely much earlier in him than it is in ordinary children. I think, therefore, we may trust the evidence of the poems, in which he speaks of his infancy and childhood, as affording a true, or but little idealised, picture of his early life. It might be unsafe to depend upon the evidence of the poems if they stood alone, but the earnestness with which he dwells upon the same topic, and repeats in prose (in his "Centuries of Meditations") what he asserts in his verse, is sufficiently convincing. I know of no author whose writings convey to the reader a stronger conviction of their author's entire sincerity and absolute truthfulness than do those of Thomas Traherne.

Traherne's "Centuries of Meditations" consists of a series of reflections on religious and moral subjects, divided into short numbered paragraphs. The manuscript (which was probably written in the last years of his life, and therefore contains his most mature thoughts) comprises four complete "Centuries," and ten numbers of a fifth "Century." From the fact that it was left unfinished it would seem that his labour upon it was cut short by his death. It was written for the benefit and instruction of a lady, a friend from whom he had received as a present the book in which it is written. It bears the following inscription on the first page :

> "This book unto the friend of my best friend,
> As of the wisest love a mark, I send,
> That she may write my Maker's praise therein,
> And make herself thereby a cherubim."

In the third "Century" of the "Meditations" we find many details of the author's infancy and childhood. I cannot do better that give the greater part of these in the author's own words :

I

Will you see the infancy of this sublime and celestial greatness? Those pure and virgin apprehensions I had in my infancy, and that divine light wherewith I was born, are the best unto this day wherein I can see the universe. By the gift of God they attended me into the world, and by His special favour I remember them till now. Verily they form the greatest gift His wisdom could bestow, for without them all other gifts had been dead and vain. They are unattainable by books, and therefore I will teach them by experience. Pray for them earnestly, for they will make you angelical and wholly celestial. Certainly Adam in Paradise had not more sweet and curious apprehensions of the world than I when I was a child.

II

All appeared new and strange at first, inexpressibly rare and delightful and beautiful. I was a little stranger which at my entrance into the world was saluted and surrounded with innumerable joys. My knowledge was Divine; I knew by intuition those things which since my apostacy I collected again by the highest reason. My very ignorance was advantageous. I seemed as one brought into the estate of innocence. All things were spotless and pure and glorious; yea, and infinitely mine and joyful and precious. I knew not that there were any sins, or complaints or laws. I dreamed not of poverties, contentions, or vices. All tears and quarrels were hidden from mine eyes. Everything was at rest, free and immortal. I

knew nothing of sickness or death or exaction.   In the absence
of these I was entertained like an angel with the works of God
in their splendour and glory ; I saw all in the peace of Eden ;
heaven and earth did sing my Creator's praises, and could not
make more melody to Adam than to me.   All Time was
Eternity, and a perpetual Sabbath.   Is it not strange that an
infant should be heir of the whole world, and see those
mysteries which the books of the learned never unfold ?

III

The corn was orient and immortal wheat which never
should be reaped nor was ever sown.   I thought it had stood
from everlasting to everlasting.   The dust and stones of the
street were as precious as gold : the gates were at first the end
of the world.   The green trees when I saw them first through
one of the gates transported and ravished me ; their sweetness
and unusual beauty made my heart to leap, and almost mad
with ecstacy, they were such strange and wonderful things.
The Men !   O what venerable and reverend creatures did the
aged seem !   Immortal Cherubims !   And young men glitter-
ing and sparkling angels, and maids strange seraphic pieces of
life and beauty !   Boys and girls tumbling in the street were
moving jewels : I knew not that they were born or should die.
But all things abided eternally as they were in their proper
places.   Eternity was manifest in the Light of the Day, and some-
thing infinite behind everything appeared, which talked with
my expectation and moved my desire.   The City seemed to

stand in Eden or to be built in Heaven. The streets were mine, the temple was mine, the people were mine, their clothes and gold and silver were mine, as much as their sparkling eyes, fair skins, and ruddy faces. The skies were mine, and so were the sun and moon and stars, and all the world was mine; and I the only spectator and enjoyer of it. I knew no churlish proprieties, nor bounds nor divisions; but all proprieties and divisions were mine, all treasures and the possessors of them. So that with much ado I was corrupted, and made to learn the dirty devices of this world, which now I unlearn, and become, as it were, a little child again that I may enter into the Kingdom of God.

These passages are succeeded in the MS. by the poem entitled " The Approach," which the reader will find at page 31 of the present volume.

In the following sections of the " Meditations " the author tells how these thoughts were first dimmed, and afterwards almost entirely lost owing to the evil influence of those around him. It is clear that his parents failed to appreciate the fact that their child was of a very uncommon type, and that the ordinary methods of dealing with children were inapplicable in his case. His early and innocent thoughts, he says, were quite obliterated by the influence of a bad education. He found that those around him were immersed in the trivial cares and vanities of common life; that they were wholly wrapped up in the outward shows of things, and were moved only by common and mercenary motives. Alas! this is the discovery that every poet makes, and it is this which constitutes the tragedy of life for him. Had any one, Traherne says, spoken to him on the great and sublime truths of God and Nature; had he been taught that God was good, and had made him the sole heir of a glorious universe; had he been assured that earth was better than gold, and water, every drop of it, a precious jewel, he would have thankfully received and gladly believed the lessons. But instead of this they tried to instil into his mind the lessons of selfishness and worldly wisdom.

IX

It was a difficult matter to persuade me that the tinseled ware upon a hobby horse was a fine thing. They did impose upon me and obtrude their gifts that made me believe a ribbon or a feather curious. I could not see where was the curiousness or fineness. And to teach me that a purse of gold was at any value seemed impossible, the art by which it becomes so, and the reasons for which it is accounted so were so deep and hidden to my inexperience. So that nature is still nearest to natural things, and farthest off from preternatural; and to esteem that the reproach of nature is an excuse in them only who are unacquainted with it. Natural things are glorious, and to know them glorious; but to call things preternatural natural monstrous. Yet all they do it who esteem gold, silver, houses, land, clothes, &c., the riches of nature, which are indeed the riches of invention. Nature knows no such riches, but art and error makes them. Not the God of Nature, but sin only was the parent of them. The riches of Nature are our souls and bodies, with all their faculties, senses, and endowments. And it had been the easiest thing in the whole world [to teach me] that all felicity consisted in the enjoyment of all the world, that it was prepared for me before I was born, and that nothing was more divine and beautiful.

Surely Traherne was here anticipating much which seems to belong to a far later date ! The doctrine here urged is in essentials the same as that which was insisted upon by Rousseau and other philosophers of the eighteenth century. Shelley himself hardly enforced the idea of the return to nature more strenuously than Traherne does in this passage. "Natural things are glorious and to know them glorious"—is not this the whole burden of Walt Whitman's poetry ? Nay, is it not the whole burden of all poetry worthy of the name ?

X

Thoughts are the most present things to thoughts, and of the most powerful influence. My Soul was only apt and disposed to great things ; but souls to souls are like apples, one being rotten rots another. When I began to speak and go, nothing began to be present to me but what was present to me in their thoughts. Nor was anything present to me any other way than it was so to them. The glass of imagination was the only mirror wherein anything was represented or appeared to me. All things were absent which they talked not of. So I began among my playfellows to prize a drum, a fine coat, a penny, a gilded book, &c., who before never dreamed of any such wealth. Goodly objects to drown all the knowledge of Heaven and Earth! As for the Heavens and Sun and Stars, they disappeared, and were no more unto me than the bare walls. So that the strange riches of man's invention quite overcame the riches of nature, being learned more laboriously and in the second place.

By this, Traherne proceeds, parents and nurses should learn the right way of teaching children. Nothing is easier than to teach the truth because the nature of the thing confirms the teaching; whereas to teach children to value "gugaus," baubles, and rattles puts false ideas into their heads, and blots out all noble and divine thoughts, rendering them uncertain about everything, and dividing them from God. "Verily," he says, "there is no savage nation under the cope of Heaven that is more absurdly barbarous than the Christian World. . . . I am sure that those barbarous people that go naked come nearer to Adam, God, and Angels in the simplicity of their wealth, though not in knowledge."

XIV

Being swallowed up therefore in the miserable gulf of idle talk and worthless vanities, thenceforth I lived among shadows, like a prodigal son feeding upon husks with swine. A comfortless wilderness full of thorns and troubles the world was or worse : a waste place covered with idleness and play, and shops, and markets, and taverns. As for churches they were things I did not understand, and schools were a burden : so that there was nothing in the world worth the having or enjoying but my game and sport, which also was a dream, and being passed wholly forgotten. So that I had wholly forgotten all goodness, bounty, comfort, and glory ; which things are the very brightness of the Glory of God, for lack of which therefore He was unknown.

XV

Yet sometimes in the midst of these dreams I should come a little to myself, so far as to feel I wanted something, secretly to expostulate with God for not giving me riches, to long after an unknown happiness, to grieve that the world was so empty and to be dissatisfied with my present state because it was vain and forlorn. I had heard of Angels and much admired that here upon earth nothing should be but dirt and streets and gutters. For as for the pleasures that were in great men's houses I had not seen them : and it was my real happiness they were unknown. For because nothing deluded me I was the more inquisitive.

XVI

Once I remember (I think I was about four years old) when
I thus reasoned with myself.   Sitting in a little obscure room
in my father's poor house : If there be a God certainly He must
be Infinite in Goodness, and that I was prompted to, by a real
whispering instinct of nature.   And if He be Infinite in Good-
ness and a perfect Being in Wisdom and Love, certainly He
must do most glorious things and give us infinite riches ; how
comes it to pass, therefore, that I am so poor ?   Of so scanty
and narrow a fortune, enjoying few and obscure comforts ?   I
thought I could not believe Him a God to me unless all His
power were employed to glorify me.   I knew not then my Soul
or Body, nor did I think of the Heavens and the Earth, the
Rivers and the Stars, the Sun or the Seas : all those were lost
and absent from me.   But when I found them made out of
nothing for me, then I had a God indeed whom I could praise
and rejoice in.

XVII

Sometimes I should be alone and without employment, when
suddenly my Soul would return to itself, and forgetting all
things in the whole world which mine eyes had seen, would be
carried away to the end of the earth, and my thoughts would
be deeply engaged with inquiries—How the Earth did end ?
Whether walls did bound it or sudden precipices ? Or whether
the Heavens by degrees did come to touch it, so that the faces
of the Earth and Heaven were so near that a man with

difficulty could creep under ?   Whatever I could imagine was inconvenient, and my reason being posed was quickly wearied. What also upheld the Earth (because it was heavy) and kept it from falling ; whether pillars or dark waters ?   And if any upheld these, what then upheld those, and what again those, of which I saw there would be no end ?   Little did I think that the Earth was round and the World so full of Beauty, Light, and Wisdom.   When I saw that, I knew by the perfection of the work there was a God, and was satisfied and rejoiced. People underneath and fields and flowers, with another Sun and another Day pleased me mightily ; but more when I knew it was the same Sun that served them by Night that served us by day.

XVIII

Sometimes I should soar above the stars, and inquire how the Heavens ended, and what was beyond them ?   Concerning which by no means could I receive satisfaction.   Sometimes my thoughts would carry me to the Creation, for I had heard now that the World which at first I had thought was Eternal had a beginning: how therefore that beginning was, and why it was ; why it was no sooner, and what was before, I mightily desired to know.   By all which I easily perceived my Soul was made to live in communion with God in all places of His dominion, and to be satisfied with the highest reason in all things.   After which it so eagerly aspired that I thought all the gold and silver in the world but dirt in comparison of satisfaction in any of these.   Sometimes I wondered why men were made no bigger ?   I would have had a man as big as a giant, a

giant as big as a castle, and a castle as big as the Heavens.
Which yet would not serve, for there was infinite space beyond
the Heavens, and all was defective and but little in comparison ;
and for man to be made infinite, I thought it would be to no
purpose, and it would be inconvenient. Why also there was not
a better Sun and better Stars, a better Sea, and better Creatures
I much admired. Which thoughts produced that poem upon
moderation which afterwards was written.

Following this the author quotes a part of the poem
he refers to, which, as it is printed on page 132, need not
be given here. The argument of his verses is that
everything is for the best and in the best possible
proportion :

"God made man greater while he made him less."

XXII

These liquid clear satisfactions were the emanations of the
highest reason, but not achieved till a long time afterwards.
In the meantime I was sometimes, though seldom, visited and
inspired with new and more vigorous desires after that Bliss
which Nature whispered and suggested to me. Every new
thing quickened my curiosity, and raised my expectation. I
remember once, the first time I came into a magnificent and
noble dining-room and was left there alone, I rejoiced to see
the gold and state and carved imagery, but when all was dead

and there was no motion, I was weary of it and departed dis-
satisfied.   But afterwards when I saw it full of lords and ladies
and music and dancing, the place which once seemed not to
differ from a solitary den had now entertainment and nothing
of tediousness in it.   By which I perceived (upon a reflection
made long after) that men and women are, when well under-
stood, a principal part of our true felicity.   By this I found
also that nothing that stood still could, by doing so, be a part
of Happiness : and that affection, though it were invisible, was
the best of motions.   But the august and glorious exercise of
virtue was more solemn and divine, which yet I saw not.   And
that all men and angels should appear in Heaven.

XXIII

Another time, in a lowering and sad evening, being alone in
the field, when all things were dead and quiet, a certain want
and horror fell upon me, beyond imagination.   The unprofit-
ableness and silence of the place dissatisfied me, its wildness
terrified me ; from the utmost ends of the earth fears surrounded
me.   How did I know but dangers might suddenly arise from
the East, and invade me from the unknown regions beyond the
seas ?   I was a weak and little child and had forgotten there
was a man alive in the earth.   Yet something also of hope and
expectation comforted me from every border.   This taught me
that I was concerned in all the world : and that in the remotest
borders the causes of peace delight me, and the beauties of
the earth, when seen, were made to entertain me : that I was

made to hold a communion with the secrets of Divine Providence in all the world : that a remembrance of all the joys I had from my birth ought always to be with me : that the presence of Cities, Temples, and Kingdoms ought to sustain me, and that to be alone in the world was to be desolate and miserable. The comfort of houses and friends, and the clear assurance of treasures everywhere, God's care and love, His Wisdom, Goodness, and Power, His Presence and watchfulness in all the ends of the earth were my strength and assurance for ever : and that those things being absent to my eye were my joys and consolations : as present to my understanding as the wideness and emptiness of the Universe which I saw before me.

XXIV

When I heard of any new Kingdom beyond the seas the light and glory of it entered into me, it rose up within me, and I was enlarged wonderfully. I entered into it, I saw its commodities, springs, meadows, riches, inhabitants, and became possessor of that new room as if it had been prepared for me, so much was I magnified and delighted in it. When the Bible was read my spirit was present in other ages. I saw the light and splendour of them, the Land of Canaan, the Israelites entering into it, the ancient glory of the Amorites, their peace and riches, their cities, houses, vines, and fig-trees, the long prosperity of their Kings, their milk and honey, their slaughter and destruction, with the joys and triumphs of God's people. All which entered into me, and God among them. I saw all

and felt all in such a lively manner as if there had been no other
way to those places but in spirit only.   This shewed me the
liveliness of interior presence, and that all ages were for most
glorious ends accessible to my understanding, yea with it, yea
within it.   For without changing place in myself I could
behold and enjoy all those.   Anything, when it was proposed,
though it was a thousand ages ago being always before me.

Some few other passages relating to Traherne's boyhood
might be quoted; but as I hope soon to publish the
"Centuries of Meditations" in complete form, it is hardly
necessary to give further extracts here.   I have quoted
enough, I trust, to create a desire in the reader's mind to
see the whole work in print.   I have found the narrative
so interesting myself that I would fain hope it will be not
less so to others.   It displays with a vividness seldom
equalled the eager, enthusiastic, thoughtful, affectionate,
and, above all, poetic character of its author.   It was
doubtless because he retained in his manhood so much of
the fresh, unspoiled, and uncorrupted spirit of his youth
that he was able to give such an engaging picture of his
early years.   It bears the stamp of veracity and sincerity
in every line ; and leaves no room in the reader's mind
(as so many autobiographies do) for the suspicion that the
author was posing himself in the most favourable light,
and suppressing the darker shades of his portraiture.   I do

not think there is anything resembling it in English literature ; nor could more than one or two other English poets have written such a narrative. It is fortunate indeed that the "Centuries of Meditations," which so narrowly escaped destruction or oblivion, should have been preserved to afford us this valuable record of the inner life of a spirit touched to such fine issues as was that of Thomas Traherne.

Turning from the brilliant illumination of our author's own account of his youthful experiences it is very disappointing to find that no information about him from external sources can be discovered before the time when he became an Oxford undergraduate. But we may, I think, conclude with little chance of error that the course of his early life was somewhat as follows : His parents, seeing the precocity and unusual promise of their child, determined to give him the best education within their power, and therefore sent him to the local Grammar School. This was founded by Bishop Gilbert in 1386. While there he must have distinguished himself so much by his good conduct and aptitude for learning that some patron—or perhaps some of his relatives who were in a better position than his father—furnished the means to enable him to proceed to Oxford and become a student there. His course at the University is thus related in the *Athenæ Oxonienses :*

Thomas Traherne, a shoemaker's son of Hereford, was entered a Commoner of Brasen-nose College on the first day of March, 1652, took one degree in Arts, left the House for a time, entered into the sacred function, and in 1661 he was actually created Master of Arts. About that time he became Rector of Credinhill, commonly called Crednell, near to the city of Hereford . . . and in 1669 Bachelor of Divinity.

To the above it may perhaps be as well to add the exact dates of the degrees bestowed upon him at the University. He was made Bachelor of Arts on October 13, 1656 ; Master of Arts on November 6, 1661 ; and Bachelor of Divinity on December 11, 1669. Why or when he "left the House for a time" does not appear ; possibly it was on account of the political troubles of the period.

When at the University we may be certain that Traherne's inclination and natural genius would lead him to study for the ministry ; and he was undoubtedly an earnest and diligent student of the history and doctrines of the Christian faith, and more especially of those of the Church of England. He found in that communion his ideal Church. We have seen that Philip Traherne, the Mayor of Hereford, was noted for his " fervent zeal for the Established Church and clergy "—and probably we shall not be wrong in thinking that the Trahernes generally were members of the English Church. That

circumstance doubtless had its influence in determining
the faith of Thomas Traherne ; but his own deeply
fervent and religious nature found in the national faith,
as George Herbert had found before him, the peace
and satisfaction which he could find nowhere else.   That
the Anglican Church can boast of having attracted to its
service such fine spirits as those of Herbert, Vaughan,
Traherne, and the many others that might be mentioned,
is surely one of its greatest honours.

We have the evidence of Antony à Wood and that of
Traherne's book entitled " Roman Forgeries " to prove
that he was an unwearied student of the antiquities of the
Church, of its Fathers, Councils, and Doctrines.   But the
best evidence on this point is to be found in the
" Advertisement to the Reader " prefixed to " Roman
Forgeries."   Herein the author gives us a lively account
of a discussion which took place between himself and a
Roman Catholic gentleman on the questions in dispute
between the two Churches.   This passage must be quoted
in full, for the story is so vividly told that the reader
becomes almost a spectator of the scene :

Before I stir further I shall add one passage which befel me
in the *Schools* as I was studying these things, and searching the
most old and authentic records in pursuance of them.   One
evening as I came out of the Bodleian Library, which is the

glory of Oxford, and this nation, at the stairs-foot I was saluted by a person that has deserved well of scholars and learning, who being an intimate friend of mine, told me there was a gentleman, his cousin, pointing to a grave person, in the quadrangle, a man that had spent many thousand pounds in promoting Popery, and that he had a desire to speak with me. The gentleman came up to us of his own accord : we agreed, for the greater liberty and privacy, to walk abroad into the New Parks.　He was a notable man, of an eloquent tongue, and competent reading, bold, forward, talkative enough ; he told me, that the Church of Rome had eleven millions of martyrs, seventeen Oecumenical Councils, above one hundred Provincial Councils, all the Doctors, all the Fathers, Unity, Antiquity, Consent, &c.　I desired him to name *one* of his eleven millions of martyrs, excepting those that died for treason in Queen Elizabeth's and King James his days : for the martyrs of the primitive times, were martyrs of the *Catholic,* but not of the *Roman* Church : they only being martyrs of the Roman Church, that die for *transubstantiation,* the *Pope's Supremacy,* the doctrine of *Merits, Purgatory,* and the like.　So many he told me they had, but I could not get him to name one.　As for his Councils, Antiquities and Fathers, I asked him what he would say, if I could clearly prove that the Church of Rome was guilty of *forging* them, so far that they had published *Canons* in the *Apostles* names, and invented *Councils* that never were, forged *letters* of Fathers, and *Decretal Epistles,* in the name of the first Bishops and Martyrs of Rome, made 5, 6, 700 years after they were dead, to the utter disguising and defacing of antiquity, for the first 480 years next after our Saviour ?　"Tush, these are

nothing but lies," quoth he, "whereby the Protestants en-
deavour to disgrace the Papists." Sir, answered I, you are a
scholar, and have heard of Isidore, Mercator, James Merlin,
Peter Crabbe, Laurentius Surius, Severinus Binius Labbè,
Cossartius, and the Collectio Regia, books of vast bulk and
price, as well as of great majesty and magnificence : you met
me this evening at the Library door ; if you please to meet me
there to-morrow morning at eight of the clock, I will take you
in ; and we will go from class to class, from book to book, and
there I will first shew in your own authors, that you publish
such instuments for good *Records :* and then prove, that those
instruments are downright frauds and forgeries ? "What hurt
is that to the Church of Rome ?" said he. No! (cried I,
amazed) Is it no hurt to the Church of Rome, to be found
guilty of *forging Canons* in the *Apostles* names, and *Epistles* in
the *Fathers'* names, which they never made ? Is it nothing in
Rome to be guilty of counterfeiting *Decrees* and *Councils,* and
Records of *Antiquity ?* *I have done with you !* whereupon I
turned from him as an obdurate person. And with this I
thought it meet to acquaint the Reader.

No other particulars of Traherne's University career are
now available, but those which I have related are
sufficient to show that it was not an unsuccessful one.
It is plain that he made his way entirely by his own
ability, for he could have had no other means of advancing
himself.

It appears from a passage in our author's "Centuries ot

Meditations" that there was at one time a conflict in his mind as to his future course in life.   He debated with himself as to whether he should pursue the path that might lead to worldly prosperity, at the cost of sacrificing or suppressing his higher aspirations, or whether he should, at the risk of poverty and obscurity, follow out the promptings of his better self.   Such a conflict, in his case, could have only one result :

When I came into the country, and being seated among silent trees and woods and hills, had all my time in mine own hands, I resolved to spend it all, whatever it cost me, in the search of Happiness, and to satiate the burning thirst which Nature had enkindled in me from my youth.   In which I was so resolute that I chose rather to live upon ten pounds a year, and to go in leather clothes and to feed upon bread and water, so that I might have all my time clearly to myself, than to keep many thousands per annum in an estate of life where my time would be devoured in care and labour.   And God was so pleased to accept of that desire that from that time to this I have had all things plentifully provided for me without any care at all, my very study of Felicity making me more to prosper than all the care in the whole world.   So that through His blessing I live a free and a kingly life, as if the world were turned again into Eden, or, much more, as it is at this day.

Truly a memorable resolution ! which has had not too

many parallels, though the failure to make it has caused many a man of fine abilities to fall into the ranks of those whom the world has conquered and subdued to its own purposes. One remembers the similar resolution of the great founder of Quakerism, which Traherne might possibly have heard of. One thinks also of Thoreau and of his life in the woods ; and of the few others who have dared to live out their own lives in their own way, regardless of the disdain or censure of the worldly-minded. That nothing but good came to Traherne from his resolution we might have been sure even if he had not himself told us so ; for what harm can come to those who are animated with such a spirit as his ? The spiritually minded derive their sustenance from the spirit, and are the richer on the ten pounds a year which Traherne speaks of than are the masters of untold wealth who are spiritually destitute.

At what period Traherne came to the decision which he has thus recorded does not appear ; but it seems probable it was at the time when, as Wood tells us, he left the University for a time. Wood places the commencement of his ministry at Credenhill at about 1661, when he was made Master of Arts. This, however, seems to be an error. Mr. E. H. W. Dunkin has kindly informed me that he has in his possession a copy of a manuscript preserved at Lambeth Library (MS. 998) containing particulars of admissions to Benefices *temp.* Common-wealth, in which the following entry appears :

Thomas Traherne, clerk, admitted 30 Dec., 1657, by the Commissioners for the Approbation of Public Preachers to the Rectory of Crednell, alias Creddenhill, Co. Hereford : patron Amabella, Countess Dowager of Kent.

In 1657 Traherne could not have been more than 21 or 22 years of age—hardly old enough, one would think, to assume entire charge of the parish.   Possibly at first he only acted as assistant to the minister whom he afterwards succeeded.

Of the course of Traherne's life at Credenhill nothing is now known, but, as far as outward events were con-cerned, it was doubtless quiet and uneventful.   He re-mained there, it would appear, for rather more than nine and a half years.   Then he was summoned to London to become private chaplain to Sir Orlando Bridgman, who, on August 30, 1667, was created Lord Keeper of the Seals.   Whether he owed his promotion to a friend's recommendation, or whether he had, before this time, become personally acquanted with Sir Orlando, we do not know, but it is certain that he must henceforth have been highly esteemed and valued by his patron.   When Bridgman was, in 1672, deprived of the Seals, and went into retirement, he still retained Traherne in his service, and it was in his patron's house at Teddington, about three months after the latter's decease, that he died. We may indeed feel certain that a mutual regard and even affection existed between them ; and perhaps it is not too great a stretch of imagination to think that the death of Traherne may have been hastened by his grief at the loss of his patron.

Sir Orlando Bridgman was not only a very able lawyer, but also an honourable, conscientious, and upright statesman. He was, perhaps, a little wanting in strength of character, and therefore appeared to his contemporaries to be something of a trimmer. He was a royalist, and remained such all through the Civil War and the Commonwealth ; though it appears that during the last years of Cromwell's reign he had in some degree made his peace with the Protector. But he was not disposed to be a mere tool in the hands of the Court party. He was made Keeper of the Seals because it was supposed that he would have been subservient to the designs of the ministry then in power ; but when it was found that he was not disposed to be a compliant tool in their hands he was dismissed from his office. He had nothing in him of a Scroggs or a Jeffries, and was therefore no fit instrument of the crew of unscrupulous and corrupt intriguers who then misruled the country. That he was of a most charitable disposition—though he has not hitherto, I believe, received credit for the fact—we have sufficient evidence. In Traherne's " Christian Ethicks " we find the following passage (p. 471): " My Lord Bridgman, late Lord Keeper, confessed himself in his Will to be but a Steward of his Estate, and prayed God to forgive all his offences in getting, mis-spending, or not spending it as he ought to do. And that after many Charitable and Pious Works, perhaps surmounting his estate tho concealed from the notice or knowledge of the world."

It has been seen from one of the extracts quoted from " Centuries of Meditations " that Traherne esteemed himself fortunate in having "all things plentifully provided for me without any care at all, my very study of Felicity making me more to prosper than all the care in the whole world." That he was perfectly sincere in this statement, and that he had all the riches and advancement he required, is certain ; but very few men, and certainly no ambitious man, under the same circumstances would have made such a declaration. To the worldly-minded his destiny must have seemed a poor, if not mean one. To be the parson of two small and obscure parishes, and the private chaplain of the Keeper of the Seals, while possessing abilities which would have adorned the highest possible station, must have seemed, to a less happily constituted temperament, a fate which would have justified much repining and discontent. That Traherne was not merely contented but happy under such circumstances is but one more proof that

> Happiness to no outward cause we owe,
> From inward sources only doth it flow.

The position of chaplain to Lord Bridgman must have brought Traherne into contact with many distinguished persons of the time ; but no trace of his intercourse with them seems now to be discoverable, save in one instance. John Aubrey, the famous gossip, to whose undiscriminating industry we are indebted for the preservation of much chaff indeed, but also for not a little precious wheat, in his " Miscellanies," under the heading "Apparitions," gives us a remarkable reference to our author. I quote the passage in full :

Mr. Trahern, B.D. (chaplain to Sir Orlando Bridgman, Lord Keeper), a learned and sober person, was son of a shoemaker in Hereford : one night as he lay in bed, the moon shining very bright, he saw the phantom of one of the apprentices, sitting in a chair in his red waistcoat, and head-band about his head, and strap upon his knee ; which apprentice was really in bed and asleep with another fellow-apprentice, in the same chamber, and saw him. The fellow was living, 1671. Another time, as he was in bed, he saw a basket come sailing in the air, along by the valence of his bed; I think he said there was fruit in the basket : it was a phantom. From him-self.

It is highly probable that it was Aubrey who furnished Wood with the account of Traherne which appears in the *Athenæ Oxonienses*, and doubtless he could have given us much more information about him had he chosen to do so. But he was incapable of appreciating so fine a spirit as Traherne's ; nor was the latter likely to reveal to him the profounder depths of his nature. It is much to be regretted that Aubrey gives us such a confused account of what he was told. The stories were doubt-less related to him at his own direct request, he being ever eager to collect accounts of the marvellous and the supernatural. It seems evident that Traherne attached little importance to these two visions, purposeless as they apparently were, and as visions of the kind usually are. No one nowadays would attribute such phantoms of the brain to any supernatural cause, nor does it appear that Traherne himself did. I find no trace in his writings of a belief in the common superstitions of his time as to ghosts, witches, or evil spirits.

The date of the interview in which Traherne related these things to Aubrey is fixed by the date given in it (1671) to a period within two or three years of the poet's death.   During these latter years he was, according to Wood, minister of the parish of Teddington, Middlesex. It was there that Sir Orlando Bridgman's country residence was situated ; and it was doubtless owing to his lordship's influence that Traherne was appointed minister.   That he did hold that position seems to be certain, though, curiously enough, his name does not appear in the list of ministers of the parish which is given in Newcourt's "Repertorium Ecclesiasticum."   Perhaps this may be accounted for by the fact that though Traherne was actually the working minister, the post was nominally held by a clerical pluralist of the time.   The succession of curates as given by Newcourt during the period of Traherne's connection with the parish is as follows : 1664, — Badcock ; 1668, Car. Bryan ; 1673, Joh. Graves ; 1677, Jacobus Elsby.

It was not until the year before his death that the first fruit of Traherne's long and laborious studies was offered to the readers of the time.   His poems—or some of them, at least—were written early in life, for he speaks of one of them as having been written "long since"; but his "Roman Forgeries," "Christian Ethicks," and "Centuries of Meditations" were almost certainly his latest productions.   Without undervaluing his two published works, it must be regretted that he did not send to the press in preference to them his poems, which would then have had the advantage of his own supervision, and would have saved his name from the total obscurity in which it has now been sunk for upwards of two centuries. But doubtless he did not anticipate so untimely an end of his career, and may well have preferred to make his first appearance in print as a serious student and thinker rather than as a poet. I feel sure that he did not undervalue his poems (what poet ever did ?) ; but he must have believed that his prose writings were better calculated to influence the world, as he desired to influence it, than they were. His "Roman Forgeries" and "Christian Ethicks" probably cost him far more labour and hard thought than his poems did ; and authors, it has been observed, usually value most highly the works which have cost them the greatest pains.

It was in 1673 that "Roman Forgeries" was published. There never was a period in the history of England when theological questions were more hotly debated than during the second half of the seventeenth century. Political and theological questions were then far more closely connected than is now the case, so that a double degree or vehemence was imparted to all the subjects of dispute which then divided the nation. Hence it was that a continual flood of partisan books and pamphlets issued from the press, to contemplate which nowadays is to be filled with a melancholy sense of the energy and intellect which our ancestors wasted in angry disputations and futile controversies.

That Traherne should have plunged into this whirlpool of controversy is, I must needs think, matter for regret. His " Roman Forgeries " is, it is true, a very able work ; and as to its main contentions a very convincing one to those who need no convincing, and possibly even to the very few Catholics who could be induced to peruse it. But most of the latter, it is probable, would brush the whole question aside, as did the Catholic gentleman whom Traherne encountered at Oxford, merely exclaiming " What does it matter ? "

As to the object of the work, the passage which I have quoted from it on p. xxxiv will give the reader a good idea of its scope and purpose. It is, in fact, an indictment of the Roman Church as being guilty of the most flagrant forgeries of documents and falsifications of historical facts for the purpose of supporting its spiritual and temporal pretensions. To those who are able to take any interest in its subject the book is by no means a dull one. Traherne, indeed, felt such a lively concern in his theme that he has succeeded in infusing much of his own animation into his pages. He deals his blows at his adversaries with such hearty good will, and has so much confidence in the justice of his cause, that the reader can hardly fail to sympathise with so earnest a combatant. Yet, as I have said, one can hardly help regretting that the book should have been written, for, well as it is done, it might have been done equally well by a writer of far inferior gifts, while it is impossible not to feel that Traherne was wasting his genius in its composition.*

Within twelve months after the publication of "Roman Forgeries" its author was dead. But he had, during the few months of life still left to him, finished another long and elaborate work. This was his "Christian Ethicks," a work of much more value and interest than his first book, though it seems to have fallen still-born from the press, and to have remained neglected and unknown ever since.

The satisfaction of seeing his second work in print was denied to its author. He had sent it to the press, but was dead before the printing of it was commenced. Sir

---

* "Roman Forgeries" must have had some popularity in its time, for it is, unlike "Christian Ethicks," a tolerably common book. Fifteen years after its publication Dean Comber, a writer of some note in his day, published a work of similar character, and with the same title. As Traherne's book was published anonymously, Dean Comber has usually received credit for that as well as for his own work. The Dean was a man of considerable ability, and he would hardly have been pleased had he been told that he would only be remembered in future times as the writer who helped himself to a striking title at the expense of one who was far superior to himself in character and genius.

Orlando died on June 25, 1674, and was interred in the church at Teddington, where a monument was erected "to him. Three months afterwards Traherne died in his patron's house, and was also buried in the church at Teddington under the reading-desk. Of the exact date of his decease we are ignorant, but he was buried on October 10, 1674.

About a fortnight before his death, Traherne sent for his friend, John Berdo, and his sister-in-law, Susan Traherne, and in their presence made his Will—a nuncupative one. This Will, which I have to thank my friend, Gordon Goodwin, for communicating to me, was registered in the Prerogative Court of Canterbury. It is a curious and interesting document, and I have therefore printed it in full in the Appendix to the present volume. From its terms, it is very evident that Traherne had accumulated no wealth, and that he died possessed of little indeed beyond his books and other personal effects.

At the time of his death Traherne was probably not more than thirty-eight years of age, but certainly under forty. He was thus in the very prime of life, and his intellect was in its fullest vigour. Had he lived he would surely have produced a succession of works which would have sensibly enriched our literature, for his industry was not less remarkable than his ability and his learning. As it was, his career must have seemed to those who were capable of appreciating his fine qualities a failure, for his books brought him little reputation ; and beyond the mention of him in the *Athenæ Oxonienses*, his name quickly sank into entire oblivion, so to remain for upwards of two centuries. A strange fate ! the strangest, perhaps, that ever befell an author of such fine genius. During all this period his manuscripts were lying unknown and neglected, and exposed to all the accidents of time and chance. Yet not altogether so, for it seems that those into whose hands his papers fell had at least a dim perception of their value. Twenty-five years after his death a little book stole into the world the title of which was as follows : " A Serious and Patheticall Contemplation of the Mercies of God, in several most Devout and Sublime Thanksgivings for the same. Published by the Reverend Doctor Hickes at the request of a friend of the Authors." It was the fortunate issue of this work of Traherne's that, after the lapse of upwards of two centuries, was to be the means of identifying him as the author of the poems contained in the present volume, which else might now be masquerading as those of Henry Vaughan. But for this we have not altogether to thank the friend of Traherne's who brought about the issue of the " Serious and Patheticall Contemplation." He certainly laid us under considerable obligations to him when he procured its publication ; but his curious idea that it was not to the purpose to tell us the author's name might have caused it to remain for ever unknown but for one clue that he gave 'us, which ultimately led to its discovery.

The "Serious and Patheticall Contemplation" opens with a letter from the Rev. George Hickes (then a well-known writer on theological subjects), in which he says that the work was recommended to him for publication by "a devout person who was a great Judge of Books ot Devotion, having given the world one already which had been well received in three impressions." He intended, he says, to have written a Preface to the book himself, but had received from a friend of the deceased author an account of him, which rendered it unnecessary for him " who can only tell how greatly the author of them wróte, but knew not how greatly he lived " to fulfil his intention. Dr. Hickes's Letter is followed by an Address " To the Reader," written by Traherne's friend. As this contains the best and most valuable account of our author which has descended to us, I need make no apology for quoting it in full :

Tho' the unhappy decay of true Piety and the Immoralities of the Age we live in may be a discouragement to the multi-plying such Books as this, yet on the other hand this degeneracy of Manners, and too evident contempt of Religion makes it (it may be) the more necessary to endeavour to retrieve the Spirit

of Devotion and the sacred Fires of Primitive Christianity.
And since 'tis hop'd this ensuing Treatise may somewhat
conduce to these noble Ends : It is thought to be no unprofit-
able undertaking to commit it to the Press, it being part of
the Remains of a very devout Christian, who is long since
removed to the Regions of Beatified Spirits, to sing those
Praises and Hallelujahs, in which he was very vigourously
employ'd whilst he dwelt amongst us : and since somewhat
of *Preface* is become, as it were, a necessary part of every book,
instead of any particular *Dedication* (which is commonly over-
stuft with Flattery and Complements) I will only give thee
some Account of the Author. To tell thee who he was, is, I
think, to no purpose : And therefore I will only tell thee what
he was, for that may possibly recommend the following Thanks-
givings and Meditations to thy use. He was a Divine of the
Church of England, of a very comprehensive Soul and very
acute Parts, so fully bent upon that Honourable Function in
which he was engaged ; and so wonderfully transported with
the Love of God to Mankind, with the excellency of those
Divine Laws which are prescribed to us, and with those in-
expressible Felicities to which we are entitled by being created
in, and redeemed to the Divine Image that he dwelt con-
tinually amongst these thoughts with great delight and satis-
faction, spending most of his time when at home in digesting
his notions of these things into writing, and was so full of
them when abroad that those who would converse with him
were forced to endure some discourse upon these subjects,
whether they had any sense of Religion or not. And therefore
to such he might be sometimes thought troublesome, but his

company was very acceptable to all such as had any inclination to Vertue and Religion. And tho' he had the misfortune to come abroad into the world in the late disordered Times, when the Foundations were cast down, and this excellent Church laid in the dust, and dissolved into Confusion and Enthusiasme ; yet his Soul was of a more refin'd alloy, and his Judgment in discerning of things more solid and considerate than to be infected with that Leaven, and therefore became much in love with the beautiful order and Primitive Devotions of this our excellent Church. Insomuch that I believe he never failed any one day either publickly or in his private Closet to make use of her publick Offices, as one part of his devotion, unless some very unavoidable business interrupted him. He was a man of a cheerful and sprightly Temper, free from anything of the sourness or formality by which some great pretenders to Piety rather disparage and misrepresent true Religion than recommend it ; and therefore was very affable and pleasant in his conversation, ready to do all good offices to his Friends, and Charitable to the Poor almost beyond his ability. But being removed out of the Country to the service of the late Lord Keeper Bridgman as his Chaplain, he died young and got early to those blissful Mansions to which he at all times aspir'd.

This eulogy of Traherne, it will be observed, was written twenty-five years after his death, when the writer could have had no possible motive to pen it, beyond a desire to do justice to the memory of his friend.

It is a most attractive picture ; but not, I am convinced,
one in which truth was sacrificed to flattery.   It is exactly
what might have been inferred from the poems and
" Centuries of Meditations " ;   but since it does not
always happen that an author's personality tallies with
that which might be deduced from his writings, it is
fortunate that the impression derived from Traherne's
works is thus confirmed by independent evidence.   The
poet was, it is plain, one of those rare and enviable
individuals in whom no jarring element is present, who
come into the world as into their rightful inheritance,
and whose whole life is a song of thankfulness for the
happiness which they enjoy in it.   His was indeed

> A happy soul that all the way
> To Heaven hath a summer's day,

and though we, who are not so constituted, and who may
question whether in a world, which to us seems to give at
least as much reason for lamenting as for rejoicing, any
man has a right to be so happy as Traherne was, the
feeling is perhaps only an outcome of that envy which
those who are tortured with a thousand doubts and mis-
givings must needs entertain for those who enjoy an
existence of entire serenity.

It is fortunate that Traherne's friend, though he did
not mention his name, yet gave us a clue to him by

mentioning that he was private chaplain to Lord Keeper Bridgeman. Without this clue we should probably have had to remain in ignorance of his authorship of the poems contained in this volume : for though there was (as will be seen later on) another clue, it was hidden away so deeply that it is unlikely it would ever have been discovered. Why Traherne's friend should have thought that it was not to the purpose to tell us who he was, and yet gave us such a means of discovering him, is rather a puzzle ; but we have reason to be ever grateful to him for what he has told us, while regretting that he has told us no more.

I must now give some account of Traherne's "Christian Ethicks." It is so rare a book that I have only just obtained a copy of it, after searching for it for nearly two years. Few books surely have had so unfortunate a fate. If there is a better book of its kind in the English language I have not been so fortunate as to meet with it. It is a work full of eloquence, persuasiveness, sagacity, and piety. While the author's concern, as might be expected, is chiefly with the spiritual life, he is by no means destitute of worldly wisdom, and he often exhibits a shrewdness and knowledge of human nature which would scarcely be expected from him. Open the book anywhere you please you can hardly fail to discover a fine thought finely expressed. How then shall we account for the fact that the work has remained in total obscurity

from the time of its first publication to the present day ?
The fact that the author died before its appearance, and
it was thus thrown into the world without a parent or
friend to foster it, was no doubt in some degree account-
able for its ill-fortune.   It is true that the author makes
no appeal to the uninstructed or the fanatical, and keeps
throughout the work upon a higher level of thought than
the generality of readers can ascend to.   He is somewhat
too fond of debating abstruse points of metaphysics, and
of dwelling upon the subtleties of theological specula-
tion.   Yet there is in the book enough, one would think,
of homely wisdom, and even of wit, to have secured it a
warm welcome from all those to whom it appealed.

I think the reader—since he is not likely to obtain a
copy of " Christian Ethicks," however much he may desire
it—will be glad to see a few extracts from it.   And first
I will quote a passage from the chapter "Of Magnanimity."
I do this because of its personal interest—for Traherne,
in painting the character of a magnanimous man, was,
whether consciously or unconsciously, drawing his own
portrait.   Flattering as the picture may seem, I do not
doubt in the least that it is a true one.

Magnanimity and contentment are very near allied ; like
brothers and sisters they spring from the same parents, but are
of several features.   Fortitude and Patience are kindred to

this incomparable virtue. Moralists distinguish Magnanimity
and Modesty, by making the one the desire of greater, the
other of less and inferior, honours. But in my apprehension
there is more in Magnanimity. It includes all that belongs to
a Great Soul : a high and mighty courage, an invincible
Patience, an immoveable Grandeur which is above the reach
of injuries, a contempt of all little and feeble enjoyments, and
a certain kind of majesty that is conversant with great things ;
a high and lofty frame of spirit, allied with the sweetness of
Courtesy and Respect ; a deep and stable resolution founded
on humility without any baseness ; an infinite hope and a vast
desire ; a Divine, profound, uncontrollable sense of one's own
capacity ; a generous confidence, and a great inclination to
heroical deeds ; all these conspire to complete it, with a severe
and mighty expectation of Bliss incomprehensible. It soars up
to Heaven, and looks down upon all dominion of fortune with
pity and disdain. Its aims and designs are transcendent to all
concerns of this little world. Its objects and its ends are
worthy of a soul that is like God in Nature ; and nothing less
than the Kingdom of God, his Life and Image ; nothing
beneath the friendship and communion with Him can be its
satisfaction. The terrors, allurements, and censures of men
are the dust of its feet : their avarice and ambition are but
feebleness before it. Their riches and contentions, and
interests and honours, but insignificant and empty trifles. All
the world is but a little bubble ; Infinity and Eternity the
only great and sovereign things wherewith it converseth. A
Magnanimous Soul is always awake. The whole globe of the
earth is but a nutshell in comparison of its enjoyments. The

sun is its lamp, the sea its fishpond, the stars its jewels, men, angels, its attendants, and God alone its sovereign delight and supreme complacency. The earth is its garden, all palaces its summer houses, cities are its cottages, empires its more spacious Courts, all ages and kingdoms its demeans, monarchs its ministers and public agents, the whole Catholick Church its family, the Eternal Son of God its pattern and example. Nothing is great if compared to a Magnanimous Soul but the sovereign Lord of all Worlds.

*   *   *   *   *

If you would have the character of a Magnanimous Soul, he is the son of Eternal Power, and the friend of Infinite Goodness, a Temple of Divine and Heavenly Wisdom, that is not imposed upon by the foul and ragged disguises of Nature, but acquainted with her great capacities and principles, more than commonly sensible of her interests, and depths, and desires. He is one that has gone in unto Felicity, and enjoyed her beauties, and comes out again her perfect Lover and Champion : a man whose inward stature is miraculous ; and his complexion so divine that he is king of as many kingdoms as he will look on : one that scorns the smutty way of enjoying things like a slave, because he delights in the celestial way, and the Image of God. He knows that all the world lies in wickedness ; and admires not at all that things palpable and near and natural, are unseen, though most powerful and glorious, because men are blind and stupid. He pities poor vicious kings that are oppressed with heavy crowns of vanity and gold, and admires how they can content themselves with such narrow territories : yet delights in their regiment of the world, and pays them the honour that is due unto them. The glorious exaltation of good kings he more abundantly extols, because so many thousand Magnanimous Creatures are committed to their trust, and they that govern them understand their value. But he sees well enough that the king's glory and true repose consists in the Catholick and Eternal kingdom. As for himself he *is come unto Mount Sion, and to the City of the Living God, the Heavenly Jerusalem, and to an innumerable company of Angels, to the General Assembly and Church of the First-born, which are written in Heaven, and to God the Judge of all, and to the spirits of iust men made perfect, and to Jesus the Mediator of the New Covenant:* and therefore receiving a Kingdom which cannot be moved, he desires to serve God acceptably with reverence and godly fear : and the truth is we can fear nothing else, for God alone is a consuming fire.

The above passage is a fairly representative one. If the reader is pleased with it, he would be equally pleased with the whole work ; if he sees nothing to admire in it, he may conclude that "Christian Ethicks" is not a book which has any message in it for him.

The following extract is taken from the chapter " Of Charity to our Neighbours " :

That which yet further commendeth this virtue of love unto us is that it is the only soul of all pleasure and felicity in all estates. It is like the light of the sun, in all the kingdoms and houses and eyes and ages, in Heaven, in earth, in the sea, in shops and temples, in schools and markets, in labours and recreations, in theatres and fable. It is *the great demon of the world*, and the sole cause of all operations. It is evidently impossible for any fancy, or play, or romance, or fable to be composed well and made delightful without a mixture of Love in the composure. In all theatres and feasts and weddings and triumphs and coronations Love is the Soul and Perfection of all. In all persons, in all occupations, in all diversions, in all labours, in all virtues, in all vices, in all occasions, in all families, in all cities and empires, in all our devotions and religious actions, Love is all in all. All the sweetness of society is seated in Love, the life of music and dancing is Love ; the happiness of houses, the enjoyment of friends, the amity of relations, the providence of kings, the allegiance of subjects, the glory of empires, the security, peace, and welfare of the world is seated in Love. Without Love all is discord and confusion. All blessings come upon us by Love, and by Love alone all delights and blessings are enjoyed. All happiness is established by Love, and by Love alone is Glory attained. God knoweth that Love uniteth Souls, maketh men of one heart in a house, fills them with liberality and kindness to each other, makes them delightful in presence, faithful in absence, tender of the honour and welfare of the beloved, apt to obey, ready to please, constant in trials, patient in sufferings, courageous in assaults, prudent in difficulties, victorious and triumphant. All that I shall need to observe further is that it *completed the Joys of Heaven*. Well, therefore, may wisdom desire Love, well may the Goodness of God delight in Love. It is the sum and glory of his Eternal Kingdom.

The following spirited, vigorous, and eloquent passage is from the chapter " Of Courage " :

What a glorious and incomparable virtue this is appeareth from the baseness and ineptitude of its contrary. A coward and an honest man can never be the same ; a coward and a constant lover can never be the same ; cowardice and wisdom are as incompatible for ever as Love and Wisdom were thought to be of old. A coward is always despicable and wretched, because he dares not expose himself to any hazards, nor adventure upon any great attempt for fear of some little pain and damage that is between him and an excellent achievement. He is baffled from the acquisition of the most great and beautiful things, and nonplust with every impediment. He is conquered before he begins to fight. The very sight of danger makes him a slave. He is undone when he sees his enemy afar off, and wounded before the point of his sword can touch his shadow. He is all ways a terror and burden to himself, a dangerous knave, and a useless creature.

Strange is the vigour in a brave man's soul. The strength of his spirit and his irresistible power, the greatness of his heart and the height of his condition, his mighty confidence and contempt of dangers, his true security and repose in himself, his liberty to dare and do what he pleaseth, his alacrity in the midst of fears, his invincible temper, are advantages which make him master of fortune. His courage fits him for all attempts, makes him serviceable to God and man, and makes him the bulwark and defence of his being and country.

Let those debauched and unreasonable men that deny the existence of virtue contemplate the reality of its excellency here, and be confounded with shame at their prodigious blindness. Their impiety designs the abolishment of Religion, and the utter extirpation of all faith, and piety, while they pretend the distinction between virtue and vice to be merely feigned for the aweing of the world, and that their names have no foundation in Nature but the craft of politicians and the traditions of their nurses. Are there no base fellows, nor brave men in the world ? Is there no difference between a Lion and a Hare ? a faint-hearted Coward and a glorious Hero ? Is there nothing brave nor vile in the world ? What is become of these Rodomontadoes wits ? Where is the boasted glory of their personal valour, if there be no difference, but courage and cowardice be the same thing ?

I have marked, I find, at least twenty other passages for quotation ; and indeed it would be easy to extract from the book enough notable sayings to form a pocket volume of religious and moral philosophy ; but I must content myself with only one other quotation. It is from the chapter " Of Knowledge " :

The sun is a glorious creature, and its beams extend to the utmost stars ; by shining on them it clothes them with light, and by its rays exciteth all their influences. It enlightens the eyes of all the creatures : it shineth on forty kingdoms at the same time, on seas and continents in a general manner ; yet so particularly regardeth all, that every mote in the air, every grain of dust, every spire of grass is wholly illuminated thereby as if it did entirely shine upon that alone. Nor does it only illuminate all these objects in an idle manner ; its beams are operative, enter in, fill the pores of things with spirits, and impregnate them with powers, cause all their emanations, odors, virtues, and operations ; springs, rivers, minerals and vegetables are all perfected by the sun ; all the motion, life and sense of birds, beasts and fishes dependeth on the same. Yet the sun is but a little spark among all the creatures that are made for the Soul ; the Soul, being the most high and noble of all, is capable of far higher perfections, far more full of life and vigour in its uses. The sphere of its activity is illimited, its energy is endless upon all its objects. It can exceed the heavens in its operations, and run out into infinite spaces. Such is the extent of knowledge that it seemeth to be the Light of all Eternity. All objects are equally near to the splendour of its beams : As innumerable millions may be conceived in its Light, with a ready capacity for millions more ; so can it penetrate all abysses, reach to the centre of all Nature, converse with all beings, visible and invisible, corporeal and spiritual, temporal and eternal, created and increated, finite and infinite, substantial and accidental, actual and possible, imaginary and real; all the mysteries of bliss and misery, all the secrets of heaven and hell are objects of the Soul's capacity, and shall be actually seen and known here.

It seems strange indeed that no compiler in search of material for a book of selections, no student in search of forgotten excellence, no seeker for wisdom conjoined with piety, has ever lighted in his search upon " Christian Ethicks." But it came into the world in a time of general dissoluteness of manners, and amid the jarrings of contending sects and the venomous contests of political parties. Probably very few copies of the book were sold, and its rarity in after times has prevented it from becoming known to any one who had the will and the power to proclaim its merits.

" Poetry," says Milton, if he be indeed the author of " Nova Solyma," " is the impetuous rush of a mind full to overflowing, strained, exalted to its utmost powers, yea, rather, lifted into ecstacy beyond itself." * Could we accept this (as we cannot) as a complete definition of the poetic faculty, we might then place Traherne in the very front rank of inspired singers. It would be impossible to give a better description of the leading characteristics of his poetry than that which we find in the words of Milton. Not Milton himself, nor even Shelley, has more of the impetuous rush of a mind lifted into ecstacy beyond itself than Traherne. No poet writes with more absolute spontaneity than he. Whatever may be wanting in him, however he may occasionally fail in

* See "Nova Solyma " : an Anonymous Romance. With Introduction, Translation, &c., by the Rev. Walter Begley. (1903.)

expression, he has always this impetuous rush, this ecstacy that rises beyond itself. A glowing ardour of conviction, a passionate spirit of love and devotion, a profound sense of the beauty and sublimity which he saw everywhere around him, a never-failing aspiration towards that Goodness which he believed to be the Fountain and the Ocean, the Beginning and the End of Things, were the sources of his inspiration, the impelling forces of his genius. Where these qualities are present their possessor can never altogether fail in expressing them, however deficient he may be in the technical accomplishments of the poet's art. These things indeed are the root, if not the flower, of all poetry worthy of the name. That Traherne was essentially a poet we might be certain even if none of his lyrical work had remained to prove it. The man who could say, " You never enjoy the world aright till the sea itself floweth in your veins, till you are clothed with the heavens, and crowned with the stars "—a sentence which contains the essence of everything that has been said by the poets who have sung of the relation between the soul of man and the spirit of Nature—did not need to write in verse in order to prove that he was beyond all question a poet. There is enough of the spirit of poetry in " Christian Ethicks " and " Centuries of Meditations " to set up a dozen versifiers. It was as impossible for Traherne to see things as a Jeremy

Bentham or a Cobbett saw them, as it was for either or
the latter to have written the sentence I have just quoted.
And who shall say that the light of imagination through
which Traherne and those who resemble him behold
the universe is a light which misleads them? Why
should we assume that those who view it with eyes
that are blind to all but its prosaic aspects are its true inter-
preters? Whatever else it may be, the universe, it is
certain, is a marvellous and stupendous poem ; and it is
singular indeed if those who are insensible to this truth
are able to see it in a clearer light than those who are
alive to all its beauty, to all its magnificence, and to all
its mystery.

With Traherne poetry was no elegant recreation, no
medium for the display of a lively fancy, no means of
exhibiting his skill as a master of metrical effects, but the
vehicle through which he expressed his deepest convic-
tions and his profoundest thoughts. He used it as a gift
which it was his duty to employ only for the highest
purposes and the most sacred ends. All that he saw, felt,
and apprehended was transmuted by the alchemy of his
mind into that mysterious union of thought, imagination,
and expression, which we half praise and half disparage
when we term it poetic inspiration. He possessed—or
rather was possessed by—that "fine madness" without
which no poet, painter, or musician ever yet created a

work which deserved to outlive its author. He saw in
the universe no "foul and pestilent congregation of
vapours," but a majestic dwelling-place for gods, angels,
and men. All nature to him was lovely and perfect;
and if the existence of evil, injustice, and sin disquieted
him for a moment he had little difficulty in persuading
himself that these things were owing not to defect or
imperfection in nature, but to the folly or perverseness of
men in departing from it. It may indeed be said of him,
as Matthew Arnold said of Wordsworth, that his eyes
refused to dwell upon the darker aspects of life and
nature; but that, in his case, as in Wordsworth's, was in a
great degree the source of his greatness, and is the reason
why he interests us. It is only those that possess an
undoubting faith who can inspire it in others. It is given
only to a Shakespeare or a Goethe to "see life steadily
and see it whole." Almost all other authors see it, as
their nature prompts them, in colours which are either
too glowing or too sombre. It has been said of the author
of "The City of Dreadful Night" that he was born that
we might have things stated at their worst, once for all:*

---

* "Nature is the great spendthrift. She will burn up the
world some day to attain what will probably seem to us a very
inadequate end; and in order to have things stated at their
worst, once for all, in English, she took a splendid genius and
made him—an army schoolmaster; starved his intellect, starved

may we not likewise say of Traherne that he was born that things might be stated, once for all, at their best? Perhaps the reader may think that his poems do not justify so strong a claim ; but when they are taken in conjunction with his " Christian Ethicks" and "Centuries of Meditations " I do not think it can be considered as an overstatement.   Whether his moral and theological views were right or wrong, Traherne at least was warranted in holding them, because they were exactly suited to his peculiar temperament, if indeed they were not the out-come of it.   Were all men blessed with so happy a disposition as his, then indeed might the world become the Eden which to him it appeared to be.   He believed that all men might be as happy as he was if they would only firmly resolve to follow the path which had led him to felicity.   Like all enthusiasts and most reformers of human nature or human institutions, he made the mistake of supposing that others were, or might be made, like-minded with himself, and did not take into account the infinite varieties of character and temperament which exist among mankind.   But to believe that men are

his heart, starved his body. All the adversity of the world smote him ; and that nothing should be wanting to her purpose Nature took care that the very sun should smite him also !   Time will avenge him : he is among the immortals."— John Davidson, in the *Speaker*, June 17, 1899.

better and nobler is at least a less fault than to believe them to be worse and baser than they are.

To claim for Traherne a place in the front rank of poets is hardly possible. Considering his limited range of subjects, we cannot put him on an equality with the poets who have exhibited more varied powers, and shown a deeper insight into human nature. But, excluding Milton, we may at least place him in the front rank of poets of his class. It is possible my opinion may be somewhat biassed by a reason which the reader will be at no loss to divine ; but I cannot help thinking that neither Herbert, Crashaw, nor Vaughan can compare with Traherne in the most essential qualities of the poet. He alone has that "impetuous rush of a mind . . . lifted into ecstasy beyond itself" which Milton, as we have seen, regarded as the chief requisite of poetry. Herbert has a finer sense of proportion, a keener perception of the importance of form and measure ; Vaughan appeals more strongly to the common sympathies of mankind ; while Crashaw, when at his best, has more fine passages of quintessential poetry, more curious felicities of expression, than Traherne ; but none of them has the vitality, the sustained enthusiasm, the power imparted by intense conviction, which we find in our author. Vitality, indeed, seems to me to be the keynote of Traherne's character. That he was

himself aware of this we may see from his poem on
Contentment :

> Employment is the very life and ground
> Of life itself ; whose pleasant motion is
>   The form of Bliss :
> All Blessedness a life with Glory crown'd ;
> Life ! Life is all : in its most full extent
> Stretcht out to all things, and with all Content.

Not, be it observed, the still life of contemplation or
inaction, but an active, eager, energetic enjoying of life,
to be so used as to get from it the utmost degree of felicity
or blessedness.   Traherne repudiates energetically the
idea that the more unhappy we make ourselves here the
greater will be our happiness hereafter.   In his " Centuries
of Meditations " he says :

> There are Christians that place and desire all their happiness
> in another life, and there is another sort of Christians that
> desire happiness in this.   The one can defer their enjoyment
> of wisdom to the world to come, and dispense with the increase
> and perfection of enjoyment for a little time ; the other are
> instant and impatient of delay, and would fain see that
> happiness here which they shall enjoy hereafter. . . . Whether
> the first sort be Christians indeed, look you to that.   They
> have much to say for themselves.   Yet certainly they that put
> off Felicity with long delays are to be much suspected.   For it

is against the nature of love and desire to defer, nor can any reason be given why they should desire it at last, and not now.

While we may not claim for Traherne's work as a whole that it is of the first order of excellence, we may, I think, make that claim for some of it. We can hardly have a better test of a poet's merits than to inquire how many of his pieces are fit to take their place in such anthologies as the "Golden Treasury," or Mr. Quiller-Couch's "Oxford Book of English Verse." Judged in this way Traherne makes, I think, a very good showing, considering (as I have elsewhere explained) that we possess only a part of his poetical works, and that what we have had probably not received his final revision. Were I asked to name the pieces which, in my opinion, deserve the honour which I have mentioned, I think my first choice would fall upon "The Salutation," "Wonder," "The Approach," "The Circulation," "Desire," "Goodness," and "On News." * I am not at all sure, however, that this is the best selection that could be made. "Innocence," "The Rapture," "Silence," "The Choice," "The Person," "The Recovery," "Love," and "Thoughts—I. and II." have perhaps equal

* This poem is included in the "Oxford Book of English Verse"; and the Rev. Orby Shipley has included two of Traherne's poems in his "Carmina Mariana."

or almost equal claims to be included in a list of Traherne's best work. But individual tastes differ so much that I daresay other readers would make another choice, for Traherne is a remarkably equal writer, and does not often fall below his own level of excellence. Yet all the poems I have mentioned, fine as they are when standing alone, gain considerably when they are read as parts of a continuous poem, the subject of which is the history of the author's progress in his pilgrimage towards the kingdom of perfect Blessedness. He too, like Bunyan's pilgrim, found difficulties and dangers in the way; but with him it was rather a triumphant progress from victory to victory than a long and bitter struggle against enemies who might at any time have overcome him. Very few of his poems dwell upon his discouragements; most of them are songs of rejoicing for victories achieved or happiness attained.

In the last analysis it will always be found that it is the poet himself and not his poetry that has the greatest interest for us. Unless he is interesting in himself he will not interest us in his writings. No amount of study and pains will suffice to render the work of a shallow and commonplace personality interesting to us. From the strong only shall sweetnesss come forth. I do not know whether I have succeeded in any degree in convincing the reader that Traherne was, both as a man

and as a poet, a very interesting character ; but if I have
not, the fault assuredly is mine, and not his. We may
study him in two aspects : firstly, as a representative of
the poetic temperament ; and secondly, as a representa-
tive of the religious idiosyncrasy in conjunction with the
poetic—for religion in many of its professors is often
enough altogether disjoined from any tincture of poetry.
In both aspects we have ample materials for studying
him : and I cannot help thinking that few writers of his
age are better worth studying.

Were Traherne a smaller man than he is, and therefore
less able to afford to have the whole truth told about
him, I should hesitate long before printing the following
remarks on some of his shortcomings. It is the less
needful to attempt to conceal his defects, since they
are for the greater part the defects of his qualities, and
therefore inseparable from them. Constituted as he was,
it was not possible for him to see things in a wholly clear
and uncoloured light. He is elevated so high above
ordinary humanity that he is unable to see clearly what
is so much beneath him. Nor is it always easy for us,
the dwellers upon the plain, to ascend to his altitude. He
is so exempt from the ordinary failings of humanity that
we feel almost as if he belonged to a different race. He
died a bachelor, and I do not find anything in his writings
which shows that he ever experienced the passion of love

in relation to the female sex. His love for the divine seems to have swallowed up all thought of sexual love, though not his love for humanity in the mass. He is sometimes so mystical or metaphysical that the ordinary reader finds it difficult to comprehend him. But, after all, if the reader will only exercise a little patience and be at the expense of a little thought, he will not find it hard to understand the poet, even in his most difficult passages. Those who are able to follow Browning through all his intricacies will find no knot in Traherne which they will not easily unravel.

The charge which is most likely to be pressed against Traherne is that he appears to have been a man of few ideas, and is consequently much given to repetition of thoughts and even of words and phrases. That there is some foundation for this charge may be admitted, but it is nevertheless unjust. No one, after the examination of his manuscripts and of his two published works, could believe it. A scholar so well versed in the classics, a student so eager for knowledge of all kinds, a thinker so acute, could not possibly be a man of narrow ideas and restricted sympathies. What is true, however, is that his mind dwelt with so much delight upon certain thoughts that it was continually recurring to them, setting them in different lights, and repeating them, even as a musician will execute ever-new variations upon a favourite theme.

Those who care for Traherne's themes will not complain that he dwells too much upon them.

It must be owned, I think, that while Traherne is usually happy in the selection of his themes, he is sometimes less happy in developing and expressing them. Lines which leave something to be desired in smoothness (though he is not usually chargeable with this fault, his handling of the heroic couplet being particularly good), and now and then lines which to our modern ideas appear to be somewhat prosaic, are certainly to be found in his poems, and do, to a small extent, interfere with the reader's pleasure in them. But for such faults as these we ought surely to make large allowance. The reader should, and doubtless will, remember that he has before him a work for which the author himself has but a limited responsibility. Had he himself published the poems we should have been entitled to think that he deliberately chose to give them to the world with all their faults upon them. As it is, I think we may assume that had he lived to publish them they would have undergone a good deal of revision before they were sent forth to the world. Most of their defects are such as might be easily remedied, and such, indeed, as it was sometimes hard to refrain from remedying. But I have resisted all such temptations, and have confined myself to the task of making the printed text as nearly as possible a reproduction

of the original manuscripts. The reader will gather from
the facsimile of one of Traherne's poems, which I have
given as a frontispiece to this volume, a good general idea
as to the character of his handwriting, his spelling, and
his punctuation. It would have been an interesting
thing could the whole of Traherne's poems have been
reproduced in the same style, for, as the reader will see,
there is a picturesqueness, a beauty, and a life about the
manuscripts which is lost in the cold regularity of type.
Some readers may perhaps think that it would have been
better to follow the author's original spelling and punctua-
tion ; but after giving full consideration to this point, it
did not seem advisable to do this. Traherne's spelling is
by no means uniform—Deity, for instance, is sometimes
" Dietie " and sometimes " Deitie "—and his punctuation,
which is, I think, quite peculiar to himself, differs so
much from our modern practice, that if it had been re-
produced without modification it would often have
obscured his meaning and puzzled the reader without
any compensating advantage.

Traherne, as will be perceived from the frontispiece,
made much use of capital letters and occasionally of italics
in his writings. This was the custom of the time, as any
one who examines a seventeenth-century printed book
will see. In the first edition of this book I preserved
most of the author's capitals and italicised passages : but

here I have thought it unnecessary to do so. Upon the whole there seemed to be no advantage in retaining them, since they look a little odd to eyes accustomed to the uniformity of modern typography. In the case of the poems taken from " Christian Ethicks," however, I have preserved the old spelling and the capitals very nearly as they appear in the book.

Traherne, so far as English authors were concerned, was very little indebted to his predecessors. He was, of course, greatly influenced by the writers of the Old and New Testaments, from whom he is continually quoting in his " Christian Ethicks." Next to the Scriptures, the book which seems most to have influenced him was that ancient mystical and philosophical work which is attributed to Hermes Trismegistus. Those who are well acquainted with that remarkable production will find frequent traces of its influence in the prose and verse of Traherne. He gives several extracts from it in " Christian Ethicks," and in his " Commonplace Book " there are continual references to it. It might almost be said that, after the Bible, it was his chief manual of philosophy and of divine wisdom.

That Traherne was well acquainted with the writings of Herbert is evident from the fact that in one of his manuscript books he has copied out that writer's poem, " To all Angels and Saints "; but I do not find any

traces of Herbert's influence upon him either in prose
or verse. Nor do I find any proof that he was acquainted
with the writings of Vaughan.   The resemblance between
Traherne's line,

> How, like an Angel came I down,

and Vaughan's reference to his "angel infancy" is probably
no more than an accidental coincidence.   Though their
points of view were similar in many respects, Traherne
possessed a much stronger personality than Vaughan, and
therefore had little or nothing to learn from him.   It is
likely enough that he owed something to Donne, as most
of the poets of his time did ; but I do not find any clear
indications of that poet's influence in his writings.
Traherne's style, indeed, is that of his age, but as to his
matter, few poets, I think, can boast of more originality.

Perhaps the most remarkable thing about Traherne's
poetry is that it anticipates so much that seems to belong
to much later periods of our literary history.   Traherne,
indeed, is likely to suffer to some extent in his reputation
because ideas which with him were certainly original—or
at least as much so as any ideas in any poets can be said
to be original—have since become commonplaces in our
literature.   The praise of the beauty and innocence of
childhood is familiar enough to us now, and has, perhaps,
in some instances been carried to a rather ridiculous

extreme. That certainly was not the case in Traherne's time. So far as I know, he was the first who dwelt upon those ideas in any other than an incidental and allusive manner. It is true that we find in Vaughan some passages of a similar tendency, but they are few and slight in comparison with those which we find in Traherne. If there are similar passages in other poets previous to, or contemporary with, the latter, I must confess that I am unacquainted with them. Nor were the poetical possibilities of the theme discovered until more than a century afterwards, when William Blake, who by the light of genius—or shall we say lunacy ?—discovered so much else, discovered them. It was fitting, indeed, that Blake, whose youthful experiences seem to have more nearly resembled Traherne's than those of any other poet, should have followed all unknowingly in the elder writer's footsteps. Had he ever sat down to record the events of his infancy and childhood, Blake's narrative, I think, however different in detail, must have been like that of his predecessor in its chief features. I do not believe that there is any point out of all those which I have quoted respecting Traherne's childhoo which Blake might not also have recorded of himself. Much as they differed in matters of faith, there was a deep and funda-mental agreement in character and temperament between the two poets. To both of them the things seen by their imaginations were more real than the things seen with the eye, and to neither of them was there any dividing line between the natural and the supernatural. Their faiths were founded upon intuition rather than reason, and they were no more troubled by doubt or disbelief than a mountain is. Their capacity for faith was infinite, and stopped short only when their imagination failed them—if it ever did fail them.

Another poet with whom Traherne has some remarkable affinities is Wordsworth—not the Wordsworth of later life, when his poetic vein, if not exhausted, had at least grown thin and unproductive, but the Wordsworth of the magnificent ode "Intimations of Immortality from Recollections of Early Childhood." Let the reader once more peruse that poem, and note carefully the leadings points in it. Then let him, bearing in mind the foregoing extracts from Traherne's "Centuries of Meditations," go carefully through the various poems in which the earlier poet celebrates the happiness of his infancy and childhood. When he has done this, let him ask himself if he would have believed that Wordsworth was unacquainted with Traherne's writings, supposing that they had been published before the later poet's time? I cannot think myself that it would have been easy in that case to think that the modern poet was entirely un-indebted to the older one. It is hardly too much to say that there is not a thought of any value in Wordsworth's Ode which is not to be found in substance in Traherne. Of course, I do not say this with any view of disparaging Wordsworth, whose Ode, even if it had been, as we know it was not, derived from Traherne, would still have been a masterpiece. Its merit, like that of Gray's "Elegy," depends at least as much upon its form as upon its substance, and that, of course, was all Words-worth's own. It is in a measure a testimony to the authentic character of their inspiration when two poets, unknown to each other, produce works which are so nearly identical in substance and spirit.

The reader will remember that Traherne in his youth determined to follow the bent of his own inclination at whatever cost of poverty or want of worldly success. That was the case also with Wordsworth. Another point in which, as it seems to me, they resembled each other was in the matter of poetic style. At first sight, indeed, there does not appear to be any likeness between them in this respect; yet, allowing for the difference in their times and their temperaments, I think we may find a good deal of similarity. Traherne's style, allowing for the nature of his subjects, is always simple and direct. His aim is to affect the minds of his readers by the weight of his thought and the enthusiasm of his utter-ance, not to astonish them by far-fetched metaphors or delight them with dulcet melodies. He has no ornament for ornament's sake, and he never attempts to clothe his " naked simple thought " in silken raiment or cloth of gold. He does not indulge in the metaphysical conceits and ingenuities with which the works of Donne and Cowley are so plentifully besprinkled. " Poetic diction " was as little sought for by him as by Wordsworth. He did not, however, fall into the error that Wordsworth sometimes did, of mistaking puerility for simplicity. I do not wish to press this point too far. I only desire to show that both poets were more solicitous about the substance than the form of their poetry. Wordsworth would have heartily endorsed the doctrine of Traherne that the best things are the commonest, and that natural objects and not artificial inventions are the true well-springs of delight.

Though the reader will, I hope, have agreed with my contention that Traherne anticipated a good many poetical ideas which have been thought to belong to much later dates, I can hardly expect him to accept without demur the claim I am now about to make on the poet's behalf. That Traherne had a considerable genius for metaphysics will be evident to any one who reads his " Christian Ethicks," or who studies at all carefully the contents of the present volume. But to claim that he was the originator of the metaphysical system

which, since it was first made known, has created more
discussion and exercised more influence than any other
has done, will probably seem at first to be a very ex-
travagant assertion. Yet that he had at least a clear
prevision of that famous system which is known as the
Berkeleian philosophy is, I think, incontestable. That
theory, it seems to me, could hardly be stated in a clearer
or more precise manner than it is in Traherne's poem
entitled " My Spirit."   I am much mistaken if the theory
of " the non-existence of independent matter," which is the
essence of Berkeley's system, is not to be found in this
poem—not, it is true, stated as a philosophical dogma,
but yet clearly implied, and not merely introduced as a
flight of poetical fancy. It seems to me that if the
following stanza from that poem is not altogether mean-
ingless, no other construction can be placed upon it than
that its author was a Berkeleian before Berkeley was
born :

> This made me present evermore
>   With whatsoe'er I saw.
> An object, if it were before
> My eyes, was by Dame Nature's law
>   Within my soul.   Her store
> Was all at once within me : all Her treasures
> Were my immediate and internal pleasures,
> Substantial joys which did inform my Mind.

With all She wrought
My Soul was fraught
And every object in my Heart a Thought
Begot or was ; I could not tell
Whether the things did there
Themselves appear,
Which in my Spirit truly seem'd to dwell ;
Or whether my conforming Mind
Were not even all that therein shin'd.

The idea that matter has no existence, apart from its existence in the Spirit of the Eternal, or in the soul of man, is surely clearly, if not positively, advanced in the last six lines of the above stanza. The thought, so strangely fascinating to a poet—and Berkeley no less than Traherne was one—that the whole exterior universe is not really a thing apart from and independent of man's consciousness of it, but something which exists only as it is perceived, is undeniably to be found in "My Spirit." I have quoted only one stanza of it, but the whole poem should be carefully studied, for it is throughout an assertion of the supremacy of mind over matter, and an averment that it is the former and not the latter which has a real existence. If it be thought that it is going too far to say that the Berkeleian system is to be found in the poem—which of course it is not as a reasoned-out and complete theory—it yet cannot be denied that it is there in germ and in such a form that it only required to be seized upon by an acute intellect to be developed in the way Berkeley developed it. That the latter knew nothing of Traherne's poem is certain, and therefore I am not attempting to detract in any way from the credit which belongs to him. I am only anxious to give the poet his due as the first who caught a glimpse of so notable a truth or error—which ever it may be.*

Deeply as Traherne was penetrated with a sense of the glory of the universe, and of the infinite greatness of its Creator, it was with no sense of abasement that he contemplated them. He felt that in his own soul, so capable of the sublimest conceptions and the most exalted aspirations, there must needs be a divine element. He was no outcast thrust out of Eden into a wilderness of spiritual destitution, but the son of a loving Father, born to a splendid inheritance, and at least as necessary to the Deity as servants and dependents are to keep up the state and dignity of a king. If God confers benefits on man it is in order that He may witness man's delight in them and

---

* It is not only in " My Spirit " that we find traces of Traherne's Berkeleianism. See the " Hymn on St. Bartholomew's Day," " The Preparative," and various passages in other poems. I do not contend, however, that we have the idea in a clear and unmistakable form anywhere but in " My Spirit."

gratitude for them. To see this is a supreme delight to Him, and without it there would be something wanting to His felicity. But I must quote a stanza from " The Recovery," lest the reader should think that I am misrepresenting the poet :

> For God enjoy'd is all His End.
> Himself He then doth comprehend
> When He is blessed, magnified,
> Extoll'd, exalted, prais'd and glorified,
> Honor'd, esteem'd, belov'd, enjoy'd,
> Admired, sanctified, obey'd,
> That is received. For *He*
> Doth place His whole Felicity
> In that, *who is despised and defied,*
> *Undeified almost if once denied.*

Matthew Arnold said of Goethe that he

> Neither made man too much a God
> Nor God too much a man.

That could hardly be said of Traherne. It is scarcely possible, I think, to deny that in the above-quoted passage he committed the fault of making " God too much a man." That, however, was a fault which he shared with most of the theologians of his time. Perhaps it is a fault which is almost inseparable from a sincere and fervent faith.   Without refining away the conception of God to a mere abstraction, it is impossible to think of Him otherwise than as an infinitely magnified and glorified man. Since the human mind is so constituted, it is surely vain to attempt to set limits within which we are to think of Him.   Every man will do this according to the law of his own temperament.   The man of cool reason and well-controlled passions will form a very different conception of the Deity from the man of enthusiastic disposition and ardent emotions.   To think of the Deity as " a power not ourselves which makes for righteousness " is no more possible for a Traherne, than it is for an Arnold to think of God as One

> who is despised and defied,
> Undeified almost if once denied.

To make all men think alike, whether on political, moral, or theological subjects, is now seen by all but a very few reactionaries to be an impossible task.   It is needless to defend Traherne for the views he took regarding the relations between God and man ; I have only thought it expedient to show that the line he followed was that to which he was impelled by the character of his individuality.

An excellent poet, a prose-writer of equal or perhaps greater excellence, an exemplary preacher and teacher, who gave in his own person an example of the virtues which he inculcated, one with whom religion was not a garment to be put on, but the life of his life and the spring of all his actions—such was Thomas Traherne. Much as I dissent from his opinions, and much as my point of view as regards the meaning and the purpose of life differs from his, I have yet found it easy to appreciate the fineness of his character, and the charm of his writings. It is not necessary that we should believe as Traherne believed in order to derive benefit from his works.   Men of all faiths may study them with profit, and derive from them a new impulse towards that "plain living and high thinking" by which alone happiness can be reached and peace of mind assured.

It remains for me to tell the strange story of the fate of Traherne's manuscripts after his death.   They passed, we may reasonably suppose, together with his books, into the hands of his brother Philip, as directed in his will. Philip Traherne, I imagine, was in some way—perhaps by marriage—connected with a family named Skipp, which dwelt at Ledbury, in Herefordshire.   These Skipps appear to have become the owners and custodians of the poet's remains ; and in their hands they probably rested down to the year 1888, when it seems that the property belonging to the family was dispersed.   Into

what hands the Traherne manuscripts then fell cannot
now be ascertained ; but it was certainly into hands that
were ignorant of their value.   In the latter part of 1896,
or the early months of 1897, some of them had de-
scended to the street bookstall, that last hope of books
and manuscripts in danger of being consigned to the
waste-paper mills.   Here, most fortunately, two of them
were discovered by my friend, Mr. William T. Brooke,
who acquired them at the price of a few pence.   They
could hardly have fallen into better hands, for Mr.
Brooke's knowledge of our poetical literature, and
especially of sacred poetry and hymnology, is no less
remarkable for its extent than for its exactness.   As soon
as he could find time to examine the manuscripts he at
once saw that they were of great interest and value.   He
could hardly imagine that writings so admirable could be
the work of an unknown author ; and he at length came
to the conclusion, from the fact that the poems resembled
those of Henry Vaughan in their subjects and partly in
their sentiments, that they must be his.   This was an
unfortunate idea, since it caused a considerable delay in
the tracing out of the real author.   Mr. Brooke com-
municated his discovery to the late Dr. Grosart, who
became so much interested in the matter that he purchased
the two manuscripts.   He, too, after some waverings of
opinion, during which he was disposed to attribute the

manuscripts, first to Theophilus Gale, and secondly to
Thomas Vaughan, became convinced that they must be
Henry Vaughan's. Under this persuasion he prepared
for the press a most elaborate edition of Vaughan's works,
in which the matter contained in the manuscripts was
to be included. This edition he was, at the time of his
death, endeavouring to find means to publish. That the
work thus projected was not actually published must, I
think, be regarded as a fortunate circumstance. Whether
the poems, on the authority of Dr. Grosart, would have
been accepted as Vaughan's, can only be conjectured ;
but it seems probable that they would, since it is unlikely
that any critic, however much he might have doubted
their imputed anthorship, would have been able to trace
out the real author. An irreparable injury would thus
have been inflicted upon Traherne, while Vaughan
would have received an unneeded accession of fame, at
the expense of puzzling all readers of a critical disposition
by the exhibition of inconsistent and irreconcilable
qualities.

Upon Dr. Grosart's death his library was purchased
by the well-known bookseller, Mr. Charles Higham, of
Farringdon Street. Included in it were the two Traherne
manuscript volumes. Having learned from Mr. Brooke
the story of the manuscripts, and that they were in Mr.
Higham's hands, I became interested in the matter, and

ultimately purchased them.   Afterwards, when a part of
Dr. Grosart's library was sold at Sotheby's, I became the
possessor of the third manuscript volume, which their
late owner appears not to have known to be Traherne's,
though nothing is needed but to compare it with the
other volumes in order to see that all three are in the
same handwriting.

It is due to Mr. Higham to say that he most liberally
allowed me to examine the manuscripts before purchasing
them, so that I might form my own opinion as to their
authorship.   I need not say that I should have been
delighted if I could have come to the same conclusion
that Mr. Brooke and Dr. Grosart had arrived at.
Inclination and interest alike impelled me to take their
view.   But when I sat down to read the poems and to
compare them with the acknowledged writings of Henry
Vaughan, I soon began to doubt, and it required but a
little time for that doubt to develop into a conviction
that whoever might have been their author, they were
assuredly not written by the Silurist.   It is true that the
poems deal, as most of Vaughan's do, solely with religious
or moral subjects, and that the author dwells continually,
as Vaughan did, upon the subjects of childhood and
innocence ; and that both authors display the same love
of nature and of a simple and natural life.   It is true also
that we find both poets making use of some rather

uncommon words and phrases, and that we find in both
the same free use of defective rhymes.   These re-
semblances, however, are merely superficial.   In all the
deeper matters of style, thought, and temperament,
Traherne and Vaughan were as far apart as any two men,
animated as both were by a deep spirit of piety and
beneficence, could well be.   To me, had there been no
other difference, one striking note of dissimilarity would
have sufficed to prove that the poems in manuscript and
those of Vaughan could not have proceeded from the
same pen.   In the manuscript poems an ever-present
quality is a passionate fervour of thought, an intense
ardour of enthusiasm, which is not to be found, or at
least only rarely, in Vaughan's works.   Restrained
emotion, expressed in verse which moves slowly and not
without effort, is, it seems to me, the leading character-
istic of Vaughan's poetry ; emotion in full flood, expressed
in lively and energetic diction, is that of Traherne's.
With Traherne all nature is bathed in warmth and light :
with Vaughan we feel sensible of a certain coolness of
temperament, and are conscious that he rejoices rather in
the twilight than in the radiance of noonday.

   With the conviction that the poems could not be
Vaughan's, while yet it seemed unlikely that they could
be the work of an altogether unknown or unpractised
writer, I began to search for indications by which their

author might possibly be discovered.   Here again I found
Mr. Brooke's assistance most valuable.   To an edition of
Giles Fletcher's " Christ's Victory and Triumph," which
he had edited, he had appended a number of previously
uncollected seventeenth-century poems.   Among these
was one entitled " The Ways of Wisdom."   To this
poem he now drew my attention, as he had previously
drawn Dr. Grosart's.   It was at once evident to me that
its style was very similar to that of the manuscript poems.
In fact, that poem, as any reader will see who cares to
study it in comparison with the other poems in this
volume, presents such strong resemblances and parallels
with them that it is hardly too much to say that the
question as to their common authorship might have been
rested entirely upon it.   However, it was of course
desirable to find further evidence.   Mr. Brooke told me
that he had found the poem in a little book in the British
Museum, entitled " A Serious and Patheticall Contempla-
tion of the Mercies of God, in several most Devout and
Sublime Thanksgivings for the same." *   The book,
Mr. Brooke also told me, contained other pieces in verse.
These I desired him to copy out.   When he had done
so it at once became evident to me that the author of the
manuscript poems and of the " Devout and Sublime

* This title was probably the invention of the publisher—
one Samuel Keble—and not of the author. ·

Thanksgivings" must be, beyond all doubt, one and the same person. The fact was as clearly demonstrated to my mind as the truths of the multiplication table. That point being settled, the next thing was to discover, if possible, who was the author of the "Devout and Sublime Thanksgivings." That might have remained unknown to the end of time, but for one clue which the book luckily afforded. This was, as the reader has seen, the statement in the "Address to the Reader" that the author was private chaplain to Sir Orlando Bridgeman. This clue had only to be patiently followed up to lead to the discovery of the author's name. This Mr. Brooke at last found to be Thomas Traherne. It was from Wood's *Athenæ Oxonienses* that the information was obtained, and from that we also learned that Traherne was the author of two books, "Roman Forgeries" and "Christian Ethicks." The next step was to examine these works to see if any evidence could be found which would connect them with the author of the manuscripts. That evidence was found in "Christian Ethicks." This was the poem which the reader will find on p. 157. The same poem, though in a shorter form and with a good many textual variations, appears in the manuscript "Centuries of Meditations" (see p. 134). Here then was proof positive that Traherne and no other was the author of the manuscripts in my possession. Though I did not require this evidence myself, it was fortunate it was found, since its discovery put the matter beyond all doubt. Will the reader accuse me of undue vanity if I say that it was with a good deal of self-satisfaction, and no little rejoicing, that I welcomed this confirmation of the opinion which I had formed solely upon critical grounds? One might be tempted to think that the whole train of circumstances by which Traherne was discovered, first to be the author of the anonymous " Thanksgivings," and through that of the more important manuscripts, has the appearance of being something more than the work of chance, were it not that their long concealment, their narrow escape from entire destruction, and the fact that the verses printed in the present volume form only a part of Traherne's poetical works, seem to forbid us to entertain such an idea.*

* From certain indications in the folio manuscript, from which the bulk of the poems in the present volume are derived, it seems clear that there must be a considerable quantity of verse by Traherne which has not yet been recovered. Appended to several poems in the folio volume are references to other poems, as, for example, at the end of " Innocence," " An Infant Eye, p. 1," and " Adam, p. 12." Other poems thus mentioned are " News," " The Odor," " The Inheritance," " The Evidence," " The Center," and " Insatiableness." As the manuscript volume containing these pieces consisted of at least 142 pages, it seems likely that the present volume con-

The manuscripts from which the contents of this book have been derived are three in number. They consist of one folio and two octavo volumes. The folio volume contains all the poems from " The Salutation " to " Goodness " which are here printed. The same volume contains a large number of prose essays and memoranda alphabetically arranged so as to form a kind of commonplace book. The greater part of these are in a handwriting which differs from Traherne's. They appear to have been written by a friend of the poet's, since Traherne has in many cases added remarks of his own to those in the other writer's handwriting. I believe it was Dr. Grosart's intention to print the whole of this material; but although it certainly has a curious interest, it does not appear to me that it is worth while to publish it at present. Some parts of this commonplace book appear to have been used as material for " Christian Ethicks " and " Centuries of Meditations " ; and the whole of it, as might be expected, is more like the notes of a student than the finished work of an essayist.

The second manuscript volume contains Traherne's

tains not more than one half of Traherne's poetical works. It may be hoped, but hardly expected, that the volume containing the poems mentioned above will some day be recovered. Possibly this mention of it may, if it still exists, lead to its eventual discovery.

"Centuries of Meditations," which I have already described and quoted largely from. The third volume contains Traherne's private religious meditations, devotions, and prayers. It is in this latter volume that the "Hymn on St. Bartholomew's Day," a facsimile of which is given as a frontispiece to the present volume, is found.

I must not conclude without thanking my friends, G. Thorn Drury and E. V. Lucas, to both of whom I am indebted for many valuable suggestions. I have also to thank the Rev. Canon Beeching for similar and not less appreciated assistance. Thanks are due also to the Rev. J. C. Foster, who drew my attention to the passage in Aubrey's " Miscellanies " relating to Traherne's visions, and to Miss Isabel Southall, who searched diligently, though without success, to find out the time and place of Traherne's birth. I have already acknowledged my obligations to Mr. W. T. Brooke, Mr. E. H. W. Dunkin, and Mr. Gordon Goodwin.

THE SALUTATION

I

THESE little limbs,
These eyes and hands which here I find,
These rosy cheeks wherewith my life begins,
   Where have ye been ? behind
What curtain were ye from me hid so long,
Where was, in what abyss, my speaking tongue ?

II

When silent I
So many thousand, thousand years
Beneath the dust did in a chaos lie,
   How could I smiles or tears,
Or lips or hands or eyes or ears perceive ?
Welcome ye treasures which I now receive.

III

I that so long
  Was nothing from eternity,
Did little think such joys as ear or tongue
   To celebrate or see:
Such sounds to hear, such hands to feel, such feet,
Beneath the skies on such a ground to meet.

IV

New burnisht joys !
  Which yellow gold and pearls excel !
Such sacred treasures are the limbs in boys,
   In which a soul doth dwell;
Their organised joints and azure veins
More wealth include than all the world contains.

V

From dust I rise,
  And out of nothing now awake,
These brighter regions which salute mine eyes,
   A gift from God I take.
The earth, the seas, the light, the day, the skies,
The sun and stars are mine ; if those I prize.

VI

Long time before
I in my mother's womb was born,
A God preparing did this glorious store,
    The world for me adorn.
Into this Eden so divine and fair,
So wide and bright, I come His son and heir.

VII

A stranger here
Strange things doth meet, strange glories see ;
Strange treasures lodg'd in this fair world appear,
    Strange all and new to me ;
But that they mine should be, who nothing was,
That strangest is of all, yet brought to pass.

WONDER

I

How like an Angel came I down !
How bright are all things here !
When first among His works I did appear
O how their Glory me did crown !
The world resembled His Eternity,
In which my soul did walk ;
And every thing that I did see
Did with me talk.

II

The skies in their magnificence,
The lively, lovely air ;
Oh how divine, how soft, how sweet, how fair !
The stars did entertain my sense,
And all the works of God, so bright and pure,
So rich and great did seem,
As if they ever must endure
In my esteem.

III

A native health and innocence
  Within my bones did grow,
And while my God did all his Glories show,
  I felt a vigour in my sense
That was all Spirit. I within did flow
    With seas of life, like wine ;
  I nothing in the world did know
    But 'twas divine.

IV

Harsh ragged objects were concealed,
    Oppressions, tears and cries,
Sins, griefs, complaints, dissensions, weeping eyes
  Were hid, and only things revealed
Which heavenly Spirits and the Angels prize.
    The state of Innocence
  And bliss, not trades and poverties,
    Did fill my sense.

V

The streets were paved with golden stones,
    The boys and girls were mine,
Oh how did all their lovely faces shine !
  The sons of men were holy ones,

In joy and beauty they appeared to me,
    And every thing which here I found,
  While like an angel I did see,
    Adorned the ground.

VI

  Rich diamond and pearl and gold
    In every place was seen ;
Rare splendours, yellow, blue, red, white and green,
  Mine eyes did everywhere behold.
Great Wonders clothed with glory did apppear,
    Amazement was my bliss,
  That and my wealth was everywhere ;
    No joy to this !

VII

  Cursed and devised proprieties,
    With envy, avarice
And fraud, those fiends that spoil even Paradise,
  Flew from the splendour of mine eyes,
And so did hedges, ditches, limits, bounds,
    I dreamed not aught of those,
  But wandered over all men's grounds,
    And found repose.

VIII

Proprieties themselves were mine
  And hedges ornaments,
Walls, boxes, coffers, and their rich contents
  Did not divide my joys, but all combine.
Clothes, ribbons, jewels, laces, I esteemed
  My joys by others worn :
For me they all to wear them seemed
  When I was born.

EDEN

I

A LEARNED and a happy ignorance
        Divided me
    From all the vanity,
From all the sloth, care, pain, and sorrow that advance
    The madness and the misery
Of men.   No error, no distraction I
Saw soil the earth or overcloud the sky.

II

I knew not that there was a serpent's sting,
        Whose poison shed
    On men, did overspread
The world ; nor did I dream of such a thing
    As sin, in which mankind lay dead.
They all were brisk and living wights to me,
Yea, pure and full of immortality.

III

Joy, pleasure, beauty, kindness, glory, love,
      Sleep, day, life, light,
    Peace, melody, my sight,
My ears and heart did fill and freely move.
    All that I saw did me delight.
The Universe was then a world of treasure,
To me an universal world of pleasure.

IV

Unwelcome penitence was then unknown,
      Vain costly toys,
    Swearing and roaring boys,
Shops, markets, taverns, coaches, were unshown ;
    So all things were that drowned my joys :
No thorns choked up my path, nor hid the face
Of bliss and beauty, nor eclipsed the place.

V

Only what Adam in his first estate,
      Did I behold ;
    Hard silver and dry gold
As yet lay under ground ; my blessed fate
    Was more acquainted with the old

And innocent delights which he did see
In his original simplicity.

VI

Those things which first his Eden did adorn
        My infancy
    Did crown.   Simplicity
Was my protection when I first was born.
      Mine eyes those treasures first did see
Which God first made.   The first effects of Love
My first enjoyments upon earth did prove ;

VII

And were so great, and so divine, so pure,
        So fair and sweet,
    So true ; when I did meet
Them here at first, they did my soul allure,
      And drew away my infant feet
Quite from the works of men ; that I might see
The glorious wonders of the Deity.

INNOCENCE

I

BUT that which most I wonder at, which most
I did esteem my bliss, which most I boast,
And ever shall enjoy, is that within
    I felt no stain nor spot of sin.

    No darkness then did overshade,
    But all within was pure and bright,
    No guilt did crush nor fear invade,
    But all my soul was full of light.

    A joyful sense and purity
        Is all I can remember,
    The very night to me was bright,
    'Twas Summer in December.

II

A serious meditation did employ
My soul within, which taken up with joy

Did seem no outward thing to note, but fly
    All objects that do feed the eye,

    While it those very objects did
    Admire and prize and praise and love,
    Which in their glory most are hid,
    Which presence only doth remove.

Their constant daily presence I
    Rejoicing at, did see,
And that which takes them from the eye
    Of others offered them to me.

III

No inward inclination did I feel
To avarice or pride ; my soul did kneel
In admiration all the day.   No lust, nor strife,
    Polluted then my infant life.

    No fraud nor anger in me mov'd
    No malice, jealousy, or spite;
    All that I saw I truly lov'd:
    Contentment only and delight

    Were in my soul.   O Heav'n ! what bliss
    Did I enjoy and feel !

What powerful delight did this
Inspire ! for this I daily kneel.

IV

Whether it be that Nature is so pure,
And custom only vicious ; or that sure
God did by miracle the guilt remove,
    And made my soul to feel his Love

    So early : or that 'twas one day,
    Wherein this happiness I found,
    Whose strength and brightness so do ray,
    That still it seems me to surround,

    Whate'er it is, it is a Light
        So endless unto me
    That I a world of true delight
    Did then, and to this day do see.

V

That prospect was the gate of Heaven, that day
The ancient Light of Eden did convey
Into my soul : I was an Adam there,
    A little Adam in a sphere

Of joys ! O there my ravisht sense
Was entertained in Paradise,
And had a sight of Innocence,
Which was beyond all bound and price.

An antepast of Heaven sure !
I on the Earth did reign,
Within, without me, all was pure :
I must become a child again.

THE PREPARATIVE

I

My body being dead, my limbs unknown ;
    Before I skill'd to prize
    Those living stars mine eyes,
Before my tongue or cheeks were to me shown,
  Before I knew my hands were mine,
Or that my sinews did my members join,
    When neither nostril, foot nor ear
As yet was seen, or felt, or did appear :
      I was within
A house I knew not, newly cloth'd with skin.

II

Then was my soul my only all to me,
    A living endless eye,
    Just bounded with the sky.
Whose power, whose act, whose essence, was to see :
  I was an inward Sphere of Light,
Or an interminable Orb of Sight,

An endless and a living day,
A vital Sun that round about did ray
  All life, all sense,
A naked simple pure Intelligence.

III

I then no thirst nor hunger did perceive,
    No dull necessity,
    No want was known to me ;
Without disturbance then I did receive
  The fair ideas of all things,
And had the honey even without the stings.
  A meditating inward eye
Gazing at quiet did within me lie,
    And every thing
Delighted me that was their heavenly King.

IV

For sight inherits beauty, hearing sounds,
    The nostril sweet perfumes,
    All tastes have hidden rooms
Within the tongue ; and feeling feeling wounds
  With pleasure and delight ; but I
Forgot the rest, and was all sight or eye :

Unbodied and devoid of care,
Just as in Heaven the holy Angels are,
    For simple sense
Is Lord of all created excellence.

V

Being thus prepared for all felicity,
    Not prepossest with dross,
    Nor stiffly glued to gross
And dull materials that might ruin me,
    Nor fettered by an iron fate
With vain affections in my earthly state
    To any thing that might seduce
My sense, or else bereave it of its use,
    I was as free
As if there were nor sin, nor misery.

VI

Pure empty powers that did nothing loath,
    Did like the fairest glass,
    Or spotless polished brass,
Themselves soon in their object's image clothe.
    Divine impressions when they came
Did quickly enter and my soul inflame.

'Tis not the object, but the light
That maketh Heaven : 'tis a purer sight.
       Felicity
Appears to none but them that purely see.

VII

A disentangled and a naked sense,
     A mind that's unpossest,
     A disengaged breast,
An empty and a quick intelligence
   Acquainted with the golden mean,
An even spirit pure and serene,
   Is that where beauty, excellence,
And pleasure keep their Court of Residence.
       My soul retire,
Get free, and so thou shalt even all admire.

THE INSTRUCTION

I

Spue out thy filth, thy flesh abjure ;
Let not contingents thee defile,
For transients only are impure,
And aery things thy soul beguile.

II

Unfelt, unseen, let those things be
Which to thy spirit were unknown,
When to thy blessed infancy
The world, thyself, thy God was shown.

III

All that is great and stable stood
Before thy purer eyes at first :
All that in visibles is good
Or pure, or fair, or unaccurst.

Whatever else thou now dost see
In custom, action, or desire,
'Tis but a part of misery
In which all men at once conspire.

THE VISION

I

FLIGHT is but the preparative. The sight
    Is deep and infinite,
Ah me ! 'tis all the glory, love, light, space,
    Joy, beauty and variety
That doth adorn the Godhead's dwelling-place,
    'Tis all that eye can see.
Even trades themselves seen in celestial light,
    And cares and sins and woes are bright.

II

Order the beauty even of beauty is,
    It is the rule of bliss,
The very life and form and cause of pleasure ;
    Which if we do not understand,
Ten thousand heaps of vain confused treasure
    Will but oppress the land.
In blessedness itself we that shall miss,
    Being blind, which is the cause of bliss.

III

First then behold the world as thine, and well
    Note that where thou dost dwell.
See all the beauty of the spacious case,
    Lift up thy pleas'd and ravisht eyes,
Admire the glory of the Heavenly place
    And all its blessings prize.
That sight well seen thy spirit shall prepare,
    The first makes all the other rare.

IV

Men's woes shall be but foils unto thy bliss,
    Thou once enjoying this :
Trades shall adorn and beautify the earth,
    Their ignorance shall make thee bright,
Were not their griefs Democritus his mirth ?
    Their faults shall keep thee right :
All shall be thine, because they all conspire,
    To feed and make thy glory higher.

V

To see a glorious fountain and an end,
    To see all creatures tend
To thy advancement, and so sweetly close
    In thy repose : to see them shine

In use, in worth, in service, and even foes
    Among the rest made thine :
To see all these unite at once in thee
    Is to behold felicity.

VI

To see the fountain is a blessed thing,
    It is to see the King
Of Glory face to face : but yet the end,
    The glorious, wondrous end is more ;
And yet the fountain there we comprehend,
    The spring we there adore :
For in the end the fountain best is shewn,
    As by effects the cause is known.

VII

From one, to one, in one to see all things,
    To see the King of Kings
But once in two ; to see His endless treasures
    Made all mine own, myself the end
Of all his labours ! 'Tis the life of pleasures !
    To see myself His friend !
Who all things finds conjoined in Him alone,
    Sees and enjoys the Holy One.

THE RAPTURE

I

SWEET Infancy !
O fire of heaven ! O sacred Light !
How fair and bright !
How great am I,
Whom all the world doth magnify !

II

O Heavenly joy !
O great and sacred blessedness
Which I possess !
So great a joy
Who did into my arms convey !

III

From God above
Being sent, the Heavens me enflame :
To praise his Name

The stars do move !
The burning sun doth shew His love.

IV

O how divine
Am I !   To all this sacred wealth,
    This life and health,
    Who raised ?   Who mine
Did make the same ?   What hand divine ?

THE IMPROVEMENT

I

'TIS more to recollect, than make. The one
Is but an accident without the other.
We cannot think the world to be the Throne
Of God, unless His Wisdom shine as Brother
   Unto His Power, in the fabric, so
   That we the one may in the other know.

II

His goodness also must in both appear,
And all the children of His love be found
In the creation of the starry sphere,
And in the forming of the fruitful ground ;
   Before we can that happiness descry
   Which is the Daughter of the deity.

III

His wisdom shines in spreading forth the sky,
His power's great in ordering the Sun,
His goodness very marvellous and high
Appears, in every work His hand hath done :

And all His works in their variety
United or asunder please the eye.

IV

But neither goodness, wisdom, power, nor love,
Nor happiness itself in things could be,
Did they not all in one fair order move,
And jointly by their service end in me :
    Had He not made an eye to be the Sphere
    Of all things, none of these would e'er appear.

V

Hie wisdom, goodness, power, as they unite,
All things in one, that they may be the treasures
Of one enjoyer, shine in the utmost height
They can attain ; and are most glorious pleasures,
    When all the universe conjoined in one,
    Exalts a creature as if that alone.

VI

To bring the moisture of far-distant seas
Into a point, to make them present here,
In virtue, not in bulk ; one man to please
With all the powers of the Highest Sphere

From East, from West, from North and South, to bring
The pleasing influence of every thing,

VII

Is far more great than to create them there
Where now they stand ; His wisdom more doth shine
In that His might and goodness more appear
In recollecting ; He is more divine
   In making every thing a gift to one
   Than in the sev'ral parts of all His spacious Throne.

VIII

Herein we see a marvellous design,
And apprehending clearly the great skill
Of that great Architect, whose love doth shine
In all His works, we find His Life and Will :
   For lively counsels do the Godhead shew,
   And these His love and goodness make us know.

IX

By wise contrivance He doth all things guide,
And so dispose them, that while they unite
For man He endless pleasures doth provide,
And shows that happiness is His delight,

His creatures' happiness as well as His :
For that in truth He seeks, and 'tis His bliss.

X

O rapture ! wonder ! ecstasie ! delight !
How great must then His glory be, how great
Our blessedness ! How vast and infinite
Our pleasure, how transcendent, how complete,
 If we the goodness of our God possess,
 And all His joy be in our blessedness.

XI

Almighty power when it is employed
For one, that He with glory might be crown'd ;
Eternal wisdom when it is enjoyed
By one whom all its pleasures do surround,
 Produce a creature that must, all his days,
 Return the sacrifice of endless praise.

XII

But Oh ! the vigour of mine infant sense
Drives me too far : I had not yet the eye,
The apprehension, or intelligence
Of things so very great, divine, and high.

But all things were eternal unto me,
And mine, and pleasing which mine eye did see.

XIII

That was enough at first : eternity,
Infinity, and love were silent joys ;
Power, wisdom, goodness, and felicity ;
All these which now our care and sin destroys,
    By instinct virtually were well discern'd,
    And by their representatives were learn'd.

XIV

As sponges gather moisture from the earth
Whereon there is scarce any sign of dew ;
As air infecteth salt : so at my birth
All these were unperceiv'd, yet near and true :
    Not by reflexion, and distinctly known,
    But by their efficacy all mine own.

THE APPROACH *

I

THAT childish thoughts such joys inspire,
Doth make my wonder and His glory higher :
His bounty and my wealth more great,
It shows His Kingdom and His Work complete :
In which there is not anything
Not meet to be the joy of Cherubim.

II

He in our childhood with us walks,
And with our thoughts mysteriously he talks ;
He often visiteth our minds,
But cold acceptance in us ever finds :
We send Him often grieved away ;
Else would He shew us all His Kingdom's joy.

* In Traherne's " Centuries of Meditations " this poem is
preceded by the following note : " Upon those pure and virgin
apprehensions which I had in my infancy I made this Poem."

III

O Lord, I wonder at Thy Love,
Which did my Infancy so early move :
 But more at that which did forbear,
And move so long, tho' slighted many a year :
 But most of all, at last that Thou
Thyself shouldst me convert I scarce know how.

IV

Thy Gracious motions oft in vain
Assaulted me : my heart did hard remain
 Long time : I sent my God away,
Grieved much that He could not impart His joy.
 I careless was, nor did regard
The end for which He all those thoughts prepar'd ;

V

But now with new and open eyes,
I see beneath as if above the skies ;
 And as I backward look again,
See all His thoughts and mine most clear and plain.
 He did approach, He me did woo ;
I wonder that my God this thing would do.

VI

From nothing taken first I was ;
What wondrous things His glory brought to pass !
    Now in this world I Him behold,
And me enveloped in more than gold;
    In deep abysses of delights,
In present hidden precious benefits.

VII

Those thoughts His goodness long before
Prepared as precious and celestial store,
    With curious art in me inlaid,
That Childhood might itself alone be said
    My tutor, teacher, guide to be,
Instructed then even by the Deity.

DUMBNESS

Sure Man was born to meditate on things,
And to contemplate the eternal springs
Of God and Nature, glory, bliss, and pleasure ;
That life and love might be his Heavenly treasure ;
And therefore speechless made at first, that He
Might in himself profoundly busied be :
And not vent out, before he hath ta'en in
Those antidotes that guard his soul from sin.

    Wise Nature made him deaf, too, that He might
Not be disturbed, while he doth take delight
In inward things, nor be deprav'd with tongues,
Nor injured by the errors and the wrongs
That mortal words convey. For sin and death
Are most infused by accursed breath,
That flowing from corrupted entrails, bear
Those hidden plagues which souls may justly fear.

    This, my dear friends, this was my blessed case ;
For nothing spoke to me but the fair face
Of Heaven and Earth, before myself could speak,
I then my Bliss did, when my silence, break.

My non-intelligence of human words
Ten thousand pleasures unto me affords ;
For while I knew not what they to me said,
Before their souls were into mine convey'd,
Before that living vehicle of wind
Could breathe into me their infected mind,
Before my thoughts were leaven'd with theirs, before
There any mixture was ; the Holy Door,
Or gate of souls was close, and mine being one
Within itself to me alone was known.
Then did I dwell within a world of light,
Distinct and separate from all men's sight,
Where I did feel strange thoughts, and such things see
That were, or seem'd, only reveal'd to me,
There I saw all the world enjoyed by one ;
There I was in the world myself alone ;
No business serious seemed but one ; no work
But one was found ; and that did in me lurk.
    D'ye ask me what ?   It was with clearer eyes
To see all creatures full of Deities ;
Especially one's self : And to admire
The satisfaction of all true desire :
'Twas to be pleased with all that God hath done ;
'Twas to enjoy even all beneath the sun :
'Twas with a steady and immediate sense
To feel and measure all the excellence

Of things ; 'twas to inherit endless treasure,
And to be filled with everlasting pleasure :
To reign in silence, and to sing alone,
To see, love, covet, have, enjoy and praise, in one :
To prize and to be ravish'd ; to be true,
Sincere and single in a blessed view
Of all His gifts.   Thus was I pent within
A fort, inpregnable to any sin :
Until the avenues being open laid
Whole legions entered, and the forts betrayed :
Before which time a pulpit in my mind,
A temple and a teacher I did find,
With a large text to comment on.   No ear
But eyes themselves were all the hearers there,
And every stone, and every star a tongue,
And every gale of wind a curious song.
The Heavens were an oracle, and spake
Divinity : the Earth did undertake
The office of a priest ; and I being dumb
(Nothing besides was dumb), all things did come
With voices and instructions ; but when I
Had gained a tongue, their power began to die.
Mine ears let other noises in, not theirs,
A noise disturbing all my songs and prayers.
My foes pulled down the temple to the ground ;
They my adoring soul did deeply wound

And casting that into a swoon, destroyed
The Oracle, and all I there enjoyed :
And having once inspired me with a sense
Of foreign vanities, they march out thence
In troops that cover and despoil my coasts,
Being the invisible, most hurtful hosts.

  Yet the first words mine infancy did hear
The things which in my dumbness did appear,
Preventing all the rest, got such a root
Within my heart, and stick so close unto 't,
It may be trampled on, but still will grow
And nutriment to soil itself will owe.
The first Impressions are Immortal all,
And let mine enemies hoop, cry, roar, or call,
Yet these will whisper if I will but hear,
And penetrate the heart, if not the ear.

SILENCE

A QUIET silent person may possess
All that is great or high in Blessedness.
The inward work is the supreme : for all
The other were occasioned by the fall.
A man that seemeth idle to the view
Of others, may the greatest business do.
Those acts which Adam in his innocence
Performed, carry all the excellence.
Those outward busy acts he knew not, were
But meaner matters of a lower sphere.
Building of churches, giving to the poor,
In dust and ashes lying on the floor,
Administering of justice, preaching peace,
Ploughing and toiling for a forct increase,
With visiting the sick, or governing
The rude and ignorant : this was a thing
As then unknown.   For neither ignorance
Nor poverty, nor sickness did advance
Their banner in the world, till sin came in.
Those therefore were occasioned all by sin.

The first and only work he had to do,
Was in himself to feel his bliss, to view
His sacred treasures, to admire, rejoice,
Sing praises with a sweet and heavenly voice,
See, prize, give hourly thanks within, and love,
Which is the high and only work above
Them all.   And this at first was mine ; these were
My exercises of the highest sphere.
To see, approve, take pleasure, and rejoice
Within, is better than an empty voice.
No melody in words can equal that ;
The sweetest organ, lute, or harp is flat
And dull, compared thereto.   And O that still
I might admire my Father's love and skill !
This is to honour, worship, and adore,
This is to love Him : nay, it is far more,
It is to enjoy Him, and to imitate
The life and glory of His high Estate.
'Tis to receive with holy reverence,
To understand His gifts, and with a sense
Of pure devotion and humility,
To prize His works, His Love to magnify.
O happy ignorance of other things
Which made me present with that King of Kings !
And like Him too !   All spirit, life, and power,
All love and joy, in His Eternal Bower,

A world of innocence as then was mine,
In which the joys of Paradise did shine :
And while I was not here I was in Heaven,
Not resting one, but every, day in seven,
For ever minding with a lively sense,
The universe in all its excellence.
No other thoughts did intervene, to cloy,
Divert, extinguish, or eclipse my joy,
No other customs, new-found wants, or dreams
Invented here polluted my pure streams,
No aloes or drugs, no wormwood star
Was seen to fall into the sea from far ;
No rotten soul, did like an apple near
My soul approach.   There's no contagion here.
An unperceived donor gave all pleasures,
There nothing was but I, and all my treasures.
In that fair world, one only was the Friend,
One golden stream, one spring, one only end.
There only one did sacrifice and sing
To only one Eternal Heavenly King.
The union was so strait between them two,
That all was either's which my soul could view :
His gifts and my possessions, both our treasures ;
He mine, and I the ocean of His pleasures.
He was an ocean of delights from Whom
The living springs and golden streams did come :

My bosom was an ocean into which
They all did run. And me they did enrich.
A vast and infinite capacity,
Did make my bosom like the Deity,
In whose mysterious and celestial mind
All ages and all worlds together shin'd,
Who tho' He nothing said did always reign,
And in Himself Eternity contain.
The world was more in me, than I in it.
The King of Glory in my soul did sit,
And to Himself in me he always gave
All that He takes delight to see me have,
For so my spirit was an endless Sphere,
Like God Himself, and Heaven, and Earth was there.

MY SPIRIT

I

My naked simple Life was I ;
   That Act so strongly shin'd
Upon the earth, the sea, the sky,
It was the substance of my mind ;
   The sense itself was I.
I felt no dross nor matter in my Soul,
No brims nor borders, such as in a bowl
We see.   My essence was capacity,
    That felt all things ;
    The thought that springs
Therefrom's itself.   It hath no other wings
  To spread abroad, nor eyes to see,
    Nor hands distinct to feel,
     Nor knees to kneel.
But being simple like the Deity
  In its own centre is a sphere
  Not shut up here, but everywhere.

II

It acts not from a centre to
　　Its object as remote,
But present is when it doth view,
Being with the Being it doth note
　　Whatever it doth do.
It doth not by another engine work,
But by itself; which in the act doth lurk.
Its essence is transformed into a true
　　　And perfect act,
　　　And so exact
Hath God appeared in this mysterious fact,
　That 'tis all eye, all act, all sight,
　　And what it please can be,
　　　Not only see,
Or do; for 'tis more voluble than light:
　Which can put on ten thousand forms,
　Being cloth'd with what itself adorns.

III

This made me present evermore
　　With whatsoe'er I saw.
An object, if it were before
My eye, was by Dame Nature's law,
　　Within my soul.　Her store

Was all at once within me ; all Her treasures
Were my immediate and internal pleasures,
Substantial joys, which did inform my mind.
  With all she wrought
  My soul was fraught,
And every object in my heart a thought
  Begot, or was ; I could not tell,
   Whether the things did there
    Themselves appear,
Which in my Spirit truly seem'd to dwell ;
  Or whether my conforming mind
  Were not even all that therein shin'd.

IV

  But yet of this I was most sure,
   That at the utmost length,
  (So worthy was it to endure)
  My soul could best express its strength.
   It was so quick and pure,
That all my mind was wholly everywhere,
Whate'er it saw, 'twas ever wholly there ;
The sun ten thousand legions off, was nigh :
   The utmost star,
   Though seen from far,
  Was present in the apple of my eye.

There was my sight, my life, my sense,
My substance, and my mind ;
My spirit shin'd
Even there, not by a transient influence :
The act was immanent, yet there :
The thing remote, yet felt even here.

V

O Joy ! O wonder and delight !
O sacred mystery !
My Soul a Spirit infinite !
An image of the Deity !
A pure substantial light !
That Being greatest which doth nothing seem !
Why, 'twas my all, I nothing did esteem
But that alone.   A strange mysterious sphere !
A deep abyss
That sees and is
The only proper place of Heavenly Bliss.
To its Creator 'tis so near
In love and excellence,
In life and sense,
In greatness, worth, and nature ; and so dear,
In it, without hyperbole,
The Son and friend of God we see.

VI

A strange extended orb of Joy,
  Proceeding from within,
Which did on every side, convey
Itself, and being nigh of kin
  To God did every way
Dilate itself even in an instant, and
Like an indivisible centre stand,
At once surrounding all eternity.
    'Twas not a sphere,
    Yet did appear,
One infinite. 'Twas somewhat everywhere,
  And tho' it had a power to see
    Far more, yet still it shin'd
    And was a mind
Exerted for it saw Infinity.
  'Twas not a sphere, but 'twas a might
  Invisible, and yet gave light.

VII

O wondrous Self ! O sphere of light,
  O sphere of joy most fair ;
O act, O power infinite ;
O subtile and unbounded air !
  O living orb of sight !

Thou which within me art, yet me ! Thou eye,
And temple of His whole infinity !
  O what a world art Thou ! A world within !
    All things appear
    All objects are
Alive in Thee ! Supersubstantial, rare,
  Above themselves, and nigh of kin
    To those pure things we find
      In His great mind
Who made the world ! Tho' now eclipsed by sin
  There they are useful and divine,
  Exalted there they ought to shine.

THE APPREHENSION

IF this I did not every moment see,
    And if my thoughts did stray
    At any time, or idly play,
    And fix on other objects, yet
      This Apprehension set
        In me
Was all my whole felicity.

FULLNESS

THAT light, that sight, that thought,
Which in my soul at first He wrought,
Is sure the only act to which I may
Assent to-day :
The mirror of an endless life,
The shadow of a virgin wife,
A spiritual world standing within,
An Universe enclosed in skin,
My power exerted, or my perfect Being,
If not enjoying, yet an act of seeing.
My bliss
Consists in this,
My duty too
In this I view.
It is a fountain or a spring,
Refreshing me in everything.
From whence those living streams I do derive,
By which my thirsty soul is kept alive.
The centre and the sphere
Of my delights are here.

It is my David's tower
Where all my armour lies,
The fountain of my power,
My bliss, my sacrifice :
A little spark
That shining in the dark,
Makes and encourages my soul to rise,
The root of hope, the golden chain,
Whose end is, as the poets feign,
Fastened to the very throne
Of Jove.
It is a stone,
On which I sit,
An endless benefit,
That being made my regal throne,
Doth prove
An Oracle of His Eternal Love.

NATURE

THAT Custom is a second Nature, we
Most plainly find by Nature's purity.
For Nature teacheth nothing but the truth ;
I'm sure that mine did in my virgin youth :
The very Day my Spirit did inspire,
The world's fair beauty set my soul on fire.
My senses were informers to my heart,
The conduits of His glory, power, and art.
His greatness, wisdom, goodness, I did see,
His glorious Love, and His Eternitie,
Almost as soon as born ; and every sense
Was in me like to some Intelligence.
I was by nature prone and apt to love
All light and beauty, both in Heaven above,
And Earth beneath, prone even to admire,
Adore, and praise as well as to desire.
My inclinations raised me up on high,
And guided me to all Infinity.
A secret self I had enclosed within,
That was not bounded with my clothes or skin,

Or terminated with my sight, the sphere
Of which was bounded with the Heavens here :
But that did rather, like the subtile light,
Secured from rough and raging storms by night,
Break through the lanthorn's sides, and freely ray
Dispersing and dilating every way :
Whose steady beams too subtile for the wind,
Are such that we their bounds can scarcely find.
It did encompass, and possess rare things,
But yet felt more, and on its angel's wings
Pierced through the skies immediately, and sought
For all that could beyond all worlds be thought.
It did not move, nor one way go, but stood,
And by dilating of itself, all good
It strove to see, as if 'twere present there,
Even while it present stood conversing here :
And more suggested than I could discern,
Or ever since by any means could learn.
Vast, unaffected wonderful desires,
Like inward, native, uncaus'd hidden fires,
Sprang up with expectations very strange,
Which into new desires did quickly change :
For all I saw beyond the azure round,
Was endless darkness with no beauty crown'd.
Why beauty should not there, as well as here,
Why goodness should not likewise there appear,

Why treasures and delights should bounded be,
Since there is such a wide Infinitie ;
These were the doubts and troubles of my Soul,
By which I do perceive without control,
A world of endless joys by Nature made,
That needs must flourish ever, never fade.
A wide, magnificent and spacious sky,
So rich 'tis worthy of the Deity,
Clouds here and there like winged charets flying,
Flowers ever flourishing, yet always dying,
A day of glory where I all things see,
As 'twere enrich'd with beams of light for me,
And drown'd in glorious rays of purer light,
Succeeded with a black, yet glorious night ;
Stars sweetly shedding to my pleased sense,
On all things their nocturnal influence,
With secret rooms in times and ages more,
Past and to come enlarging my great store :
These all in order present unto me
My happy eyes did in a moment see,
With wonders there-too, to my Soul unknown,
Till they by men and reading first were shewn.
All which were made that I might ever be
With some great workman, some Great Deity.
But yet there were new rooms and spaces more,
Beyond all these, new regions o'er and o'er,

Into all which my pent-up Soul like fire
Did break, surmounting all I here admire.
The spaces fill'd were like a cabinet
Of joys before me most distinctly set :
The empty like to large and vacant room
For fancy to enlarge in, and presume
A space for more, remov'd, but yet adorning
Those near at hand, that pleased me every morning.
Here I was seated to behold new things,
In the fair fabric of the King of Kings.
All, all was mine.   The fountain tho' not known,
Yet that there must be one was plainly shewn,
Which fountain of delights must needs be Love,
As all the goodness of the things did prove.
It shines upon me from the highest skies,
And all its creatures for my sake doth prize,
Of whose enjoyment I am made the end,
While how the same is so I comprehend.

EASE

I

How easily doth Nature teach the soul
How irresistible is her infusion !
There's nothing found that can her force control
But sin. How weak and feeble's all delusion !

II

Things false are forc'd and most elaborate,
Things pure and true are obvious unto sense ;
The first impressions in our earthly state
Are made by things most great in excellence.

III

How easy is it to believe the sky
Is wide and great and fair ! How soon may we
Be made to know the Sun is bright and high,
And very glorious, when its beams we see !

IV

That all the Earth is one continued globe,
And that all men therein are living treasures,
That fields and meadows are a glorious robe
Adorning it with smooth and heavenly pleasures.

V

That all we see is ours, and every one
Possessor of the whole ; that every man
Is like a God Incarnate on the Throne,
Even like the first for whom the world began ;

VI

Whom all are taught to honour, serve, and love,
Because he is belov'd of God unknown ;
And therefore is on Earth itself above
All others, that His wisdom might be shewn.

VII

That all may happy be, each one most blest,
Both in himself and others ; all most high,
While all by each, and each by all possest
Are intermutual joys beneath the sky.

VIII

This shows a wise contrivance, and discovers
Some great Creator sitting on the Throne,
That so disposeth things for all His lovers,
That every one might reign like God alone.

SPEED

I

THE liquid pearl in springs,
The useful and the precious things
Are in a moment known.
Their very glory does reveal their worth
   (And that doth set their glory forth);
As soon as I was born they all were shewn.

II

True living wealth did flow
In crystal streams below
My feet, and trilling down
In pure, transparent, soft, sweet, melting pleasures,
   Like precious and diffusive treasures,
At once my body fed, and soul did crown.

III

I was as high and great
As Kings are in their seat.

All other things were mine.
The world my house, the creatures were my goods,
   Fields, mountains, valleys, woods,
Men and their arts to make me rich combine.

IV

   Great, lofty, endless, stable,
   Various and Innumerable,
   Bright, useful, fair, divine.
Immovable and sweet the treasures were,
   The sacred objects did appear
More rich and beautiful, as well as mine.

V

   New all ! new-burnisht joys ;
   Tho' now by other toys
   Eclipst : new all and mine.
Great Truth so sacred seemed for this to me,
   Because the things which I did see
Were such, my state I knew to be divine.

VI

   Nor did the Angels' faces,
   The glories and the graces,

The beauty, peace and joy
Of Heaven itself, more sweetness yield to me.
　Till filthy sin did all destroy
Those were the offspring of the Deity.

THE CHOICE

I

WHEN first Eternity stoop'd down to nought
And in the Earth its likeness sought,
When first it out of nothing fram'd the skies,
And form'd the moon and sun
That we might see what it had done,
It was so wise,
That it did prize
Things truly greatest, brightest, fairest, best,
All which it made, and left the rest.

II

Then did it take such care about the Truth,
Its daughter, that even in her youth,
Her face might shine upon us, and be known,
That by a better fate,
It other toys might antedate
As soon as shewn ;
And be our own,

While we were hers ; and that a virgin love
Her best inheritance might prove.

III

Thoughts undefiled, simple, naked, pure ;
Thoughts worthy ever to endure,
Our first and disengaged thoughts it loves,
And therefore made the truth,
In infancy and tender youth
So obvious to
Our easy view
That it doth prepossess our Soul, and proves
The cause of what it all ways moves.

IV

By merit and desire it doth allure ;
For truth is so divine and pure,
So rich and acceptable, being seen,
(Not parted, but in whole)
That it doth draw and force the soul,
As the great Queen
Of bliss, between
Whom and the Soul, no one pretender ought
Thrust in to captivate a thought.

V

Hence did Eternity contrive to make
　　The truth so fair for all our sake
That being truth, and fair and easy too,
　　　While it on all doth shine,
　　We might by it become divine,
　　　　Being led to woo
　　　　The thing we view,
And as chaste virgins early with it join,
　　That with it we might likewise shine.

VI

Eternity doth give the richest things
　　To every man, and makes all Kings.
The best and richest things it doth convey
　　　To all, and every one,
　　It raised me unto a throne !
　　　　Which I enjoy,
　　　　In such a way,
That truth her daughter is my chiefest bride,
　　Her daughter truth's my chiefest pride.

VII

All mine !　And seen so easily !　How great, how blest !
　　How soon am I of all possest !

My infancy no sooner opes its eyes,
But straight the spacious Earth
Abounds with joy, peace, glory, mirth,
And being wise
The very skies,
And stars do mine become ; being all possest
Even in that way that is the best.

THE PERSON

I

Ye Sacred limbs,
A richer blazon I will lay
    On you than first I found :
    That like celestial kings,
Ye might with ornaments of joy
    Be always crown'd.
A deep vermilion on a red,
On that a scarlet I will lay,
    With gold I'll crown your head,
    Which like the Sun shall ray.
With robes of glory and delight
    I'll make you bright.
Mistake me not, I do not mean to bring
    New robes, but to display the thing :
Nor paint, nor clothe, nor crown, nor add a ray,
But glorify by taking all away.

II

The naked things
Are most sublime, and brightest show,
    When they alone are seen :
    Men's hands than Angels' wings
Are truer wealth even here below :
    For those but seem.
Their worth they then do best reveal,
When we all metaphors remove,
    For metaphors conceal,
    And only vapours prove.
They best are blazon'd when we see
    The anatomy,
Survey the skin, cut up the flesh, the veins
    Unfold : the glory there remains :
The muscles, fibres, arteries, and bones
Are better far than crowns and precious stones.

III

Shall I not then
Delight in those most sacred treasures
    Which my great Father gave,
    Far more than other men

Delight in gold?   Since these are pleasures
That make us brave !
Far braver than the pearl and gold
That glitter on a lady's neck !
The rubies we behold,
The diamonds that deck
The hands of queens, compared unto
The hands we view ;
The softer lilies and the roses are
Less ornaments to those that wear
The same, than are the hands, and lips and eyes
Of those who those false ornaments so prize.

IV

Let verity
Be thy delight ; let me esteem
True wealth far more than toys :
Let sacred riches be,
While falser treasures only seem,
My real joys.
For golden chains and bracelets are
But gilded manacles, whereby
Old Satan doth ensnare,
Allure, bewitch the eye.
Thy gifts, O God, alone I'll prize,
My tongue, my eyes,

My cheeks, my lips, my ears, my hands, my feet ;
    Their harmony is far more sweet ;
Their beauty true.   And these in all my ways
Shall themes become and organs of Thy praise.

THE ESTATE

I

But shall my soul no wealth possess,
    No outward riches have ?
Shall hands and eyes alone express
    Thy bounty ? Which the grave
Shall strait devour. Shall I become
    Within myself a living tomb
Of useless wonders ? Shall the fair and brave
And great endowments of my soul lie waste,
Which ought to be a fountain, and a womb
    Of praises unto Thee ?
    Shall there no outward objects be,
      For these to see and taste ?
Not so, my God, for outward joys and pleasures
Are even the things for which my limbs are treasures.

II

My palate is a touch-stone fit
  To taste how good Thou art,
And other members second it
  Thy praises to impart.
There's not an eye that's fram'd by Thee,
  But ought Thy life and love to see :
Nor is there, Lord, upon mine head an ear,
But that the music of Thy works should hear.
Each toe, each finger, framed by Thy skill,
  Ought ointments to distil.
Ambrosia, nectar, wine should flow
  From every joint I owe,
Or things more rich ; while they Thy holy will
Are instruments adapted to fulfill.

III

They ought, my God, to be the pipes
  And conduits of Thy praise.
Men's bodies were not made for stripes,
  Nor anything but joys.
They were not made to be alone :
  But made to be the very throne
Of Blessedness, to be like Suns, whose rays,
  Dispersed, scatter many thousand ways.

They drink in nectars, and disburse again
    In purer beams, those streams,
  Those nectars which are caus'd by joys,
    And as the spacious main
Doth all the rivers, which it drinks, return,
Thy love receiv'd doth make the soul to burn.

IV

Elixirs richer are than dross,
    And ends are more divine
Than are the means ; but dung and loss
    Materials (tho' they shine
Like gold and silver) are, compar'd
    To what Thy Spirit doth regard,
Thy will require, Thy love embrace, Thy mind
Esteem, Thy nature most illustrious find.
These are the things wherewith we God reward.
    Our love He more doth prize,
  Our gratitude is in His eyes
    Far richer than the skies.
And those affections which we do return,
Are like the love which in Himself doth burn.

V

We plough the very skies, as well
    As earth ; the spacious seas

Are ours ; the stars all gems excel.
The air was made to please
The souls of men : devouring fire
Doth feed and quicken man's desire.
The orb of light in its wide circuit moves,
Corn for our food springs out of very mire,
Our fuel grows in woods and groves ;
Choice herbs and flowers aspire
To kiss our feet : beasts court our loves.*
How glorious is man's fate !
The laws of God, the works He did create,
His ancient ways, are His and my Estate.

* These five lines have an alternative reading :

The Sun itself doth in its glory shine,
And gold and silver out of very mire,
And pearls and rubies out of earth refine ;
While herbs and flowers aspire
To touch and make our feet divine.

THE ENQUIRY

I

MEN may delighted be with springs,
While trees and herbs their senses please,
And taste even living nectar in the seas :
    May think their members things
Of earthly worth at least, if not divine,
And sing because the earth for them doth shine :

II

But can the Angels take delight,
  To see such faces here beneath ?
Or can perfumes indeed from dung-hills breathe ?
    Or is the world a sight
Worthy of them ? Then may we mortals be
Surrounded with eternal Clarity.

III

Even holy angels may come down
    To walk on Earth, and see delights,
That feed and please, even here, their appetites.
        Our joys may make a crown
For them.   And in His Tabernacle men may be
Like palms we mingled with the Cherubs see.

IV

Men's senses are indeed the gems,
    Their praises the most sweet perfumes,
Their eyes the thrones, their hearts the Heavenly rooms,
        Their souls the diadems,
Their tongues the organs which they love to hear,
Their cheeks and faces like to theirs appear.

V

The wonders which our God hath done,
    The glories of His attributes,
Like dangling apples or like golden fruits,
        Angelic joys become.
His wisdom shines on Earth ; His love doth flow,
Like myrrh or incense, even here below.

VI

And shall not we such joys possess,
  Which God for man did chiefly make?
The Angels have them only for our sake!
    And yet they all confess
His glory here on Earth to be divine,
And that His Godhead in His works doth shine.

THE CIRCULATION

I

As fair ideas from the sky,
   Or images of things,
Unto a spotless mirror fly,
   On unperceived wings,
And lodging there affect the sense,
   As if at first they came from thence ;
While being there, they richly beautify
  The place they fill, and yet communicate
  Themselves, reflecting to the seer's eye ;
   Just such is our estate.
  No praise can we return again,
  No glory in ourselves possess,
But what derived from without we gain,
From all the mysteries of blessedness.

II

No man breathes out more vital air
  Than he before sucked in :

Those joys and praises must repair
To us, which 'tis a sin
To bury in a senseless tomb.
An earthly wight must be the heir
Of all those joys the holy Angels prize,
He must a king before a priest become,
And gifts receive or ever sacrifice.
'Tis blindness makes us dumb :
Had we but those celestial eyes,
Whereby we could behold the sum
Of all His bounties, we should overflow
With praises did we but their causes know.

III

All things to Circulations owe
Themselves ; by which alone
They do exist ; they cannot shew
A sigh, a word, a groan,
A colour or a glimpse of light,
The sparkle of a precious stone,
A virtue, or a smell, a lovely sight,
A fruit, a beam, an influence, a tear,
But they another's livery must wear,
And borrow matter first,
Before they can communicate.
Whatever's empty is accurst :

And this doth shew that we must some estate
Possess, or never can communicate.

IV

A sponge drinks in the water, which
Is afterwards exprest.
A liberal hand must first be rich :
Who blesseth must be blest.
The thirsty earth drinks in the rain,
The trees suck moisture at their roots,
Before the one can lavish herbs again,
Before the other can afford us fruits.
No tenant can raise corn or pay his rent,
Nor can even have a lord,
That has no land.   No spring can vent,
No vessel any wine afford
Wherein no liquor's put.   No empty purse,
Can pounds or talents of itself disburse.

V

Flame that ejects its golden beams
Sups up the grosser air ;
To seas that pour out their streams
In springs, those streams repair ;
Receiv'd ideas make even dreams.
No fancy painteth foul or fair

But by the ministry of inward light,
That in the spirits cherisheth its sight.
The moon returneth light, and some men say
The very sun no ray
Nor influence could have, did it
No foreign aids, no food admit.
The earth no exhalations would afford,
Were not its spirits by the sun restored.

VI

All things do first receive, that give :
Only 'tis God above,
That from and in Himself doth live ;
Whose all-sufficient love
Without original can flow
And all the joys and glories shew
Which mortal man can take delight to know.
He is the primitive eternal spring
The endless ocean of each glorious thing.
The soul a vessel is,
A spacious bosom, to contain
All the fair treasures of His bliss,
Which run like rivers from, into the main,
And all it doth receive returns again.

AMENDMENT

I

THAT all things should be mine,
This makes His bounty most divine :
But that they all more rich should be,
And far more brightly shine,
As used by me ;
It ravisheth my soul to see the end,
To which this work so wonderful doth tend.

II

That we should make the skies
More glorious far before Thine eyes
Than Thou didst make them, and even Thee
Far more Thy works to prize,
As used they be
Than as they're made, is a stupendous work,
Wherein Thy wisdom mightily doth lurk.

III

Thy greatness, and Thy love,
Thy power, in this, my joy doth move ;
Thy goodness, and felicity
  . In this exprest above
    All praise I see :
While Thy great Godhead over all doth reign,
And such an end in such a sort attain.

IV

What bound may we assign,
O God, to any work of thine !
Their endlessness discovers thee
    In all to be Divine ;
     A Deity
That will for evermore exceed the end
Of all that creature's wit can comprehend.

V

Am I a glorious spring
Of joys and riches to my King ?
Are men made Gods ?   And may they see
    So wonderful a thing
     As God in me ?

And is my soul a mirror that must shine
Even like the sun and be far more divine ?

VI

Thy Soul, O God, doth prize
The seas, the earth, our souls, the skies ;
As we return the same to Thee
They more delight Thine eyes,
And sweeter be
As unto thee we offer up the same,
Than as to us from Thee at first they came.

VII

O how doth Sacred Love
His gifts refine, exalt, improve !
Our love to creatures makes them be
In Thine esteem above
Themselves to Thee !
O here His goodness evermore admire !
He made our souls to make His creatures higher.

THE DEMONSTRATION

I

THE highest things are easiest to be shewn,
And only capable of being known.
   A mist involves the eye
   While in the middle it doth live ;
   And till the ends of things are seen
The way's uncertain that doth stand between.
   As in the air we see the clouds
   Like winding sheets or shrouds,
   Which, though they nearer are, obscure
The sun, which, higher far, is far more pure.

II

Its very brightness makes it near the eye,
Tho' many thousand leagues beyond the sky.
   Its beams by violence
   Invade, and ravish distant sense.
   Only extremes and heights are known,
No certainty, where no perfection's, shewn.

Extremities of blessedness
Compel us to confess
A God indeed, Whose excellence
In all His works must needs exceed all sense.

III

And for this cause incredibles alone
May be by demonstration to us shewn.
Those things that are most bright
Sun-like appear in their own light,
And nothing's truly seen that's mean :
Be it a sand, an acorn, or a bean,
It must be cloth'd with endless glory,
Before its perfect story
(Be the spirit ne'er so clear)
Can in its causes and its ends appear.

IV

What can be more incredible than this,
Where may we find a more profound abyss ?
What Heavenly height can be
Transcendent to this Summity !
What more desirable object can
Be offered to the soul of hungering man !

His gifts as they to us come down
  Are infinite and crown
The soul with strange fruitions ; yet
Returning from us they more value get.

V

And what than this can be more plain and clear ?
What truth than this more evident appear ?
    The Godhead cannot prize
  The sun at all, nor yet the skies,
  Or air, or earth, or trees, or seas,
Or stars, unless the soul of man they please.
  He neither sees with human eyes,
    Nor needs Himself seas, skies,
  Or earth, or any thing : He draws
No breath, nor eats or drinks by Nature's laws.

VI

The joy and pleasure which His soul doth take
In all His works is for His creatures' sake.
    So great a certainty
  We in this holy doctrine see
  That there could be no worth at all
In any thing material, great, or small,

Were not some creature more alive,
Whence it might worth derive.
God is the spring whence things come forth,
Souls are the fountains of their real worth.

VII

The joy and pleasure which His soul doth take
In all His works is for His creatures' sake.
Yet doth He take delight
That's altogether infinite
In them even as they from Him come,
For such His love and goodness is, the sum
Of all His happiness doth seem,
At least in His esteem,
In that delight and joy to lie
Which is His blessed creatures' melody.

VIII

In them He sees, and feels, and smells, and lives,
In them affected is to whom He gives :
In them ten thousand ways,
He all His work again enjoys
All things from Him to Him proceed
By them : are His in them : as if indeed

His Godhead did itself exceed.
To them He all conveys;
Nay, even Himself ! He is the End
To whom in them Himself, and all things tend.

THE ANTICIPATION

I

My contemplation dazzles in the End
        Of all I comprehend,
        And soars above all heights,
Diving into the depths of all delights.
        Can He become the End,
        To whom all creatures tend,
Who is the Father of all Infinites?
Then may He benefit receive from things,
And be not Parent only of all springs.

II

The End doth want the means, and is the cause,
        Whose sake, by Nature's laws,
        Is that for which they are.
Such sands, such dangerous rocks we must beware :
        From all Eternity
        A perfect Deity

Most great and blessed he doth still appear ;
His essence perfect was in all its features,
He ever blessed in His joys and creatures.

III

From everlasting He those joys did need,
    And all those joys proceed
    From Him eternally.
From everlasting His felicity
    Complete and perfect was,
    Whose bosom is the glass,
Wherein we all things everlasting see.
His name is Now, His Nature is Forever :
None can His creatures from their Maker sever.

IV

The End in Him from everlasting is
    The fountain of all bliss :
    From everlasting it
Efficient was, and influence did emit,
    That caused all. Before
    The world, we do adore
This glorious End. Because all benefit
From it proceeds : both are the very same,
The End and Fountain differ but in Name.

V

That so the End should be the very Spring
Of every glorious thing ;
And that which seemeth last,
The fountain and the cause ; attained so fast
That it was first ; and mov'd
The Efficient, who so lov'd
All worlds and made them for the sake of this ;
It shews the End complete before, and is
A perfect token of His perfect bliss.

VI

The End complete, the means must needs be so,
By which we plainly know,
From all Eternity,
The means whereby God is, must perfect be.
God is Himself the means
Whereby He doth exist :
And as the Sun by shining's cloth'd with beams,
So from Himself to all His glory streams,
Who is a Sun, yet what Himself doth list.

VII

His endless wants and His enjoyments be
From all Eternity

Immutable in Him :
They are His joys before the Cherubim.
His wants appreciate all,
And being infinite,
Permit no being to be mean or small
That He enjoys, or is before His sight :
His satisfactions do His wants delight.

VIII

Wants are the fountains of Felicity ;
No joy could ever be
Were there no want.   No bliss,
No sweetness perfect were it not for this.
Want is the greatest pleasure
Because it makes all treasure.
O what a wonderful profound abyss
Is God !   In whom eternal wants and treasures
Are more delightful, since they both are pleasures.

IX

He infinitely wanteth all His joys ;
(No want the soul e'er cloys.)
And all those wanted pleasures
He infinitely hath.   What endless measures,
What heights and depths may we
In His felicity

Conceive!   Whose very wants are endless pleasures.
His life in wants and joys is infinite,
And both are felt as His Supreme Delight.

X

He's not like us ; possession doth not cloy,
      Nor sense of want destroy ;
      Both always are together ;
No force can either from the other sever.
      Yet there's a space between
      That's endless.   Both are seen
Distinctly still, and both are seen for ever.
As soon as e'er He wanteth all His bliss,
His bliss, tho' everlasting, in Him is.

XI

His Essence is all Act : He did that He
      All Act might always be.
      His nature burns like fire ;
His goodness infinitely does desire
      To be by all possesst ;
      His love makes others blest.
It is the glory of His high estate,
And that which I for evermore admire,
He is an Act that doth communicate.

XII

From all to all Eternity He is
    That Act : an Act of bliss :
    Wherein all bliss to all
That will receive the same, or on him call,
    Is freely given : from whence
    'Tis easy even to sense
To apprehend that all receivers are
In Him, all gifts, all joys, all eyes, even all
At once that ever will or shall appear.

XIII

He is the means of them, they not of Him.
    The Holy Cherubim,
    Souls, Angels from Him came
Who is a glorious bright and living Flame,
    That on all things doth shine,
    And makes their face divine.
And Holy, Holy, Holy is His Name :
He is the means both of Himself and all,
Whom we the Fountain, Means, and End do call.

THE RECOVERY

I

To see us but receive, is such a sight
As makes His treasures infinite !
Because His goodness doth possess
In us, His own, and our own Blessedness.
Yea more, His love doth take delight
To make our glory infinite ;
Our blessedness to see
Is even to the Deity
A Beatific vision ! He attains
His Ends while we enjoy. In us He reigns.

II

For God enjoy'd is all His End.
Himself He then doth comprehend
When He is blessed, magnified,
Extoll'd, exalted, prais'd, and glorified,
Honor'd, esteem'd, belov'd, enjoy'd,
Admired, sanctified, obeyed,

That is received. For He
Doth place His whole felicity
In that : who is despised and defied,
Undeified almost if once denied.

III

In all His works, in all His ways,
We must His glory see and praise ;
And since our pleasure is the end,
We must His goodness, and His love attend.
If we despise His glorious works,
Such sin and mischief in it lurks
That they are all made vain ;
And this is even endless pain
To Him that sees it : Whose diviner grief
Is hereupon (ah me !) without relief.

IV

We please His goodness that receive :
Refusers Him of all bereave.
As bridegrooms know full well that build
A palace for their bride. It will not yield
Any delight to him at all
If she for whom he made the hall

Refuse to dwell in it,
    Or plainly scorn the benefit.
Her act that's woo'd yields more delight and pleasure
If she receives, than all the pile of treasure.

V

But we have hands, and lips, and eyes,
    And hearts and souls can sacrifice ;
    And souls themselves are made in vain
If we our evil stubbornness retain.
    Affections, praises, are the things
    For which He gave us all those springs ;
        They are the very fruits
        Of all those trees and roots,
The fruits and ends of all His great endeavours,
Which He abolisheth whoever severs.

VI

'Tis not alone a lively sense,
    A clear and quick intelligence,
    A free, profound, and full esteem ;
Tho' these elixirs all and ends do seem :
    But gratitude, thanksgiving, praise,
    A heart returned for all those joys,

These are the things admired,
These are the things by Him desired :
These are the nectar and the quintessence,
The cream and flower that most affect His sense.

VII

The voluntary act whereby
These are repaid is in His eye
More precious than the very sky.
All gold and silver is but empty dross,
Rubies and sapphires are but loss,
The very sun, and stars and seas
Far less His spirit please :
One voluntary act of love
Far more delightful to His soul doth prove,
And is above all these as far as love.

ANOTHER

I

HE seeks for ours as we do seek for His ;
Nay, O my Soul, ours is far more His bliss
Than His is ours ; at least it so doth seem
        Both in His own and our esteem :

II

His earnest love, His infinite desires,
His living, endless, and devouring fires,
Do rage in thirst and fervently require
        A love 'tis strange it should desire.

III

We cold and careless are, and scarcely think
Upon the glorious spring whereat we drink.
Did He not love us we could be content :
        We wretches are indifferent !

IV

He courts our love with infinite esteem,
And seeks it so that it doth almost seem
Even all His blessedness.　His love doth prize
　　It as the only Sacrifice.

V

'Tis death, my soul, to be indifferent,
Set forth thyself unto thy whole extent,
And all the glory of His passion prize,
　　Who for thee lives, who for thee dies.

VI

His goodness made thy love so great a pleasure,
His goodness made thy soul so great a treasure
To thee and Him : that thou mightst both inherit,
　　Prize it according to its merit.

VII

There is no goodness nor desert in thee,
For which thy love so coveted should be ;
His goodness is the fountain of thy worth ;
　　O live to love and set it forth.

VIII

Thou nothing giv'st to Him, He gave all things
To thee, and made thee like the King of Kings:
His love the fountain is of Heaven and Earth,
    The cause of all thy joy and mirth.

IX

Thy love is nothing but itself, and yet
So infinite is His that He doth set
A value infinite upon it.   Oh!
    This, canst thou careless be, and know !

X

Let that same goodness, which being infinite,
Esteems thy love with infinite delight,
Tho' less than His, tho' nothing, always be
    An object infinite to thee.

XI

And as it is the cause of all esteem,
Of all the worth which in thy love doth seem,
So let it be the cause of all thy pleasure,
    Causing its being and its treasure.

LOVE

I

O NECTAR ! O delicious stream !
O ravishing and only pleasure !   Where
    Shall such another theme
Inspire my tongue with joys or please mine ear !
    Abridgment of delights !
      And queen of sights !
O mine of rarities ! O Kingdom wide !
O more ! O cause of all ! O glorious Bride !
    O God ! O Bride of God ! O King !
    O soul and crown of everything !

II

    Did not I covet to behold
Some endless monarch, that did always live
    In palaces of gold,
Willing all kingdoms, realms, and crowns to give
    Unto my soul ! Whose love
      A spring might prove

Of endless glories, honors, friendships, pleasures,
Joys, praises, beauties and celestial treasures !
  Lo, now I see there's such a King,
  The fountain-head of everything !

III

  Did my ambition ever dream
Of such a Lord, of such a love !   Did I
    Expect so sweet a stream
As this at any time !   Could any eye
      Believe it ?   Why all power
      Is used here ;
Joys down from Heaven on my head do shower,
And Jove beyond the fiction doth appear
    Once more in golden rain to come
    To Danæ's pleasing fruitful womb.

IV

  His Ganimede ! His life ! His Joy !
Or He comes down to me, or takes me up
    That I might be His boy,
And fill, and taste, and give, and drink the cup.
      But those (tho' great) are all
      Too short and small,

Too weak and feeble pictures to express
The true mysterious depths of Blessedness.
   I am His image, and His friend,
   His son, bride, glory, temple, end.

THOUGHTS.—I

I

YE brisk, divine and living things,
Ye great exemplars, and ye heavenly springs,
    Which I within me see ;
      Ye machines great,
   Which in my spirit God did seat,
    Ye engines of felicity ;
Ye wondrous fabrics of His hands,
Who all possesseth that He understands ;
    That ye are pent within my breast,
    Yet rove at large from East to West,
And are invisible, yet infinite,
Is my transcendent and my best delight.

II

    By you I do the joys possess
Of yesterday's-yet-present blessedness ;
      As in a mirror clear,
       Old objects I
    Far distant do even now descry,
    Which by your help are present here.

Ye are yourselves the very pleasures,
The sweetest, last, and most substantial treasures :
The offsprings and effects of bliss
By whose return my glory is
Renew'd and represented to my view :
O ye delights, most pure, divine, and true !

III

Ye thoughts and apprehensions are
The Heavenly streams which fill the soul with rare
Transcendent perfect pleasures.
At any time
As if ye still were in your prime,
Ye open all His heavenly treasures.
His joys accessible are found
To you, and those things enter which surround
The soul.   Ye living things within !
Where had all joy and glory been
Had ye not made the soul those things to know,
Which seated in it make the fairest shew ?

IV

I know not by what secret power
Ye flourish so : but ye within your bower

More beautiful do seem,
    And better meat
Ye daily yield my soul to eat,
Than even the objects I esteem
Without my soul. , What were the sky,
What were the sun, or stars, did ye not lie
    In me, and represent them there
    Where else they never could appear !
Yea, what were bliss without such thoughts to me,
What were my life, what were the Deity ?

V

O ye Conceptions of delight !
Ye that inform my soul with life and light !
    Ye representatives, and springs
    Of inward pleasure !
Ye joys, ye ends of outward treasure !
Ye inward and ye living things !
The thought or joy conceived is
The inward fabric of my standing bliss :
    It is the very substance of my mind
    Transform'd and with its objects lined,
The quintessence, elixir, spirit, cream :
'Tis strange that things unseen should be supreme.

VI

The eye's confined, the body's pent
In narrow room : limbs are of small extent,
But thoughts are always free ;
And as they're best
So can they even in the breast
Rove o'er the world with liberty :
Can enter ages, present be
In any kingdom, into bosoms see.
Thoughts, thoughts can come to things and view
What bodies can't approach unto :
They know no bar, denial, limit, wall,
But have a liberty to look on all.

VII

Like bees they fly from flower to flower,
Appear in every closet, temple, bower,
And suck the sweet from thence
No eye can see :
As tasters to the Deity,
Incredible their excellence,
For evermore they will be seen,
Nor ever moulder into less esteem.

They ever shew an equal face,
And are immortal in their place :
Ten thousand Ages hence they are as strong,
Ten thousand Ages hence they are as young.

THOUGHTS.—II

I

A DELICATE and tender thought
The quintessence is found of all He wrought;
  It is the fruit of all his works,
    Which we conceive,
    Bring forth, and give,
Yea and in which the greater value lurks.
  It is the fine and curious flower
Which we return and offer every hour;
  So tender is our Paradise
    That in a trice
  It withers strait and fades away
If we but cease its beauty to display.

II

Why things so precious should be made
So prone, so easy, and so apt to fade
  It is not easy to declare;
    But God would have
    His creatures brave,
And that too by their own continual care.

He gave them power every hour
Both to erect and to maintain a tower,
  Which he far more in us doth prize
    Than all the skies,
  That we might offer it to Him,
And in our souls be like the Seraphim.

III

That temple David did intend
Was but a thought, and yet it did transcend
  King Solomon's.   A thought we know
    Is that for which
    God doth enrich
With joys even Heaven above and Earth below.
  For that all objects might be seen
He made the orient azure and the green :
  That we might in his works delight
    And that the sight
  Of those His treasures might enflame
The soul with love to Him, He made the same.

IV

This sight which is the glorious End
Of all His works and which doth comprehend

Eternity and time and space,
  Is far more dear,
  And far more near
To Him, than all His glorious dwelling-place.
  It is a spiritual world within,
A living world and nearer far of kin
   To God than that which first he made.
   While that doth fade
  This therefore ever shall endure
Within the soul as more divine and pure.

[THE INFLUX]

I

YE hidden nectars, which my God doth drink,
    Ye heavenly streams, ye beams divine,
        On which the angels think,
    How quick, how strongly do ye shine !
Ye images of joy that in me dwell,
        Ye sweet mysterious shades
      That do all substances excel,
        Whose glory never fades ;
Ye skies, ye seas, ye stars, or things more fair,
O ever, ever unto me repair !

II

Ye pleasant thoughts !   O how that sun divine
    Appears to-day which I did see
      So sweetly then to shine
    Even in my very infancy !

Ye rich ideas which within me live
   Ye living pictures here,
  Ye spirits that do bring and give
    All joys ; when ye appear
Even Heaven itself and God, and all in you
Come down on earth and please my blessed view.

III

I never glorious great and rich am found,
  Am never ravished with joy,
    Till ye my soul surround :
   Till ye my blessedness display
No soul but stone, no man but clay am I,
   No flesh, but dust, till ye
  Delight, invade and move my eye,
   And do replenish me ;
My sweet informers and my living treasures,
My great companions and my only pleasures !

IV

O what incredible delights, what fires,
  What appetites, what joys do ye
   Occasion, what desires,
  What heavenly praises !   While we see
What every Seraphim above admires !

Your Jubilee and trade,
Ye are so strangely and divinely made,
Shall never, never fade :
Ye ravish all my soul : Of you I twice
Will speak, for in the dark y'are Paradise.

THOUGHTS.—III

THOUGHTS are the Angels which we send abroad,
To visit all the parts of God's abode.
Thoughts are the things wherein we all confess
The quintessence of sin and holiness
Is laid.   All wisdom in a thought doth shine,
By thoughts alone the soul is made divine.
Thoughts are the springs of all our actions here
On earth, tho' they themselves do not appear.
They are the springs of beauty, order, peace,
The city's gallantries, the fields' increase.
Rule, government, and kingdoms flow from them,
And so doth all the New Jerusalem,
At least the glory, splendour, and delight,
For 'tis by thoughts that even she is bright.
Thoughts are the things wherewith even God is crown'd,
And as the soul without them's useless found,
So are all other creatures too.   A thought
Is even the very cream of all He wrought.

All holy fear, and love, and reverence,
With honour, joy, and praise, as well as sense,
Are hidden in our thoughts.   Thoughts are the things
That us affect : The honey and the stings
Of all that is are seated in a thought,
Even while it seemeth weak, and next to nought.
The matter of all pleasure, virtue, worth,
Grief, anger, hate, revenge, which words set forth,
Are thoughts alone.   Thoughts are the highest things,
The very offspring of the King of Kings.
Thoughts are a kind of strange celestial creature
That when they're good, they're such in every feature.
They bear the image of their Father's face,
And beautify even all His dwelling-place :
So nimble, volatile, and unconfined,
Illimited, to which no form's assigned,
So changeable, capacious, easy, free,
That what itself doth please a thought may be.
From nothing to infinity it turns,
Even in a moment : Now like fire it burns,
Now's frozen ice : Now shapes the glorious sun,
Now darkness in a moment doth become.
Now all at once : Now crowded in a sand,
Now fills the hemisphere, and sees a land :
Now on a sudden's wider than the sky,
And now runs parile with the Deity.

'Tis such that it may all or nothing be,
And's made so active, voluble, and free
Because 'tis capable of all that's good,
And is the end of all when understood.
A thought can clothe itself with all the treasures
Of God, and be the greatest of His pleasures.
It all His laws, and glorious works, and ways,
And attributes and counsels, all His praise
It can conceive and imitate, and give :
It is the only being that doth live.
'Tis capable of all perfection here,
Of all His love and joy and glory there.
It is the only beauty that doth shine,
Most great, transcendent, heavenly, and divine.
The very best or worst of things it is,
The basis of all misery or bliss.
Its measures and capacities are such,
Their utmost measure we can never touch.
Here ornament on ornament may still
Be laid ; beauty on beauty, skill on skill,
Strength still on strength, and life itself on life,
'Tis Queen of all things, and its Maker's wife.
The best of thoughts is yet a thing unknown,
But when 'tis perfect it is like His own :
Intelligible, endless, yet a sphere
Substantial too : In which all things appear,

All worlds, all excellencies, senses, graces,
Joys, pleasures, creatures, and the angels' faces.
It shall be married ever unto all,
And all embrace, tho' now it seemeth small.
A thought my soul may omnipresent be,
For all it toucheth which a thought can see.
O that mysterious Being !   Thoughts are things
Which rightly used make His creatures Kings.

DESIRE

I

FOR giving me desire,
An eager thirst, a burning ardent fire,
A virgin infant flame,
A Love with which into the world I came,
An inward hidden heavenly love,
Which in my soul did work and move,
And ever ever me inflame
With restless longing, heavenly avarice,
That never could be satisfied,
That did incessantly a Paradise
Unknown suggest, and something undescried
Discern, and bear me to it ; be
Thy Name for ever praised by me.

II

My parched and withered bones
Burnt up did seem : my soul was full of groans :
My thoughts extensions were :
Like paces, reaches, steps they did appear :

They somewhat hotly did pursue,
Knew that they had not all their due,
    Nor ever quiet were :
But made my flesh like hungry, thirsty ground,
    My heart a deep profound abyss,
And every joy and pleasure but a wound,
So long as I my Blessedness did miss.
    O Happiness ! A famine burns,
    And all my life to anguish turns !

III

    Where are the silent streams,
The living waters and the glorious beams,
    The sweet reviving bowers,
The shady groves, the sweet and curious flowers,
    The springs and trees, the heavenly days,
    The flow'ry meads, and glorious rays,
    The gold and silver towers ?
Alas ! all these are poor and empty things !
    Trees, waters, days, and shining beams,
Fruits, flowers, bowers, shady groves and springs,
No joy will yield, no more than silent streams ;
    Those are but dead material toys,
    And cannot make my heavenly joys.

IV

O Love !   Ye amities,
And friendships that appear above the skies !
Ye feasts and living pleasures !
Ye senses, honours, and imperial treasures !
Ye bridal joys ! ye high delights
That satisfy all appetites !
Ye sweet affections, and
Ye high respects !   Whatever joys there be
In triumphs, whatsoever stand
In amicable sweet society,
Whatever pleasures are at His right hand,
Ye must before I am divine,
In full propriety be mine.

V

This soaring, sacred thirst,
Ambassador of bliss, approached first,
Making a place in me
That made me apt to prize, and taste, and see.
For not the objects but the sense
Of things doth bliss to souls dispense,
And make it, Lord, like thee.

Sense, feeling, taste, complacency, and sight,
   These are the true and real joys,
The living, flowing, inward, melting, bright,
And heavenly pleasures ; all the rest are toys :
   All which are founded in Desire,
   As light in flame and heat in fire.

THOUGHTS.—IV

In Thy presence there is fullness of Joy, and at Thy right hand there are pleasures for evermore.

THOUGHTS are the wings on which the soul doth fly,
The messengers which soar above the sky,
Elijah's fiery chariot, that conveys
The soul, even here, to those eternal joys.
Thoughts are the privileged posts that soar
Unto His throne, and there appear before
Ourselves approach.   These may at any time
Above the clouds, above the stars may climb.
The soul is present by a thought; and sees
The New Jerusalem, the palaces,
The thrones, and feasts, the regions of the sky,
The joys and treasures of the Deity.
His wisdom makes all things so bright and pure,
That they are worthy ever to endure.
His glorious works, His laws and counsels are,
When seen, all like Himself, beyond compare.

All ages with His love and glory shine,
As they are His all Kingdoms are Divine.
Whole hosts of Angels at His throne attend,
And joyful praises from His saints ascend.
Thousands of thousands kneel before His face
And all His benefits with joy embrace.
His goodness makes all creatures for His pleasure,
And makes itself His creatures' chiefest treasure.
Almighty power doth itself employ
In all its works to make itself the joy
Of all His hosts, and to complete the bliss
Which omnipresent and eternal is.
His omnipresence is an Endless Sphere,
Wherein all worlds as his delights appear :
His bounty is the spring of all delight ;
Our blessedness, like His, is infinite.
His glory endless is and doth surround
And fill all worlds without or end or bound.
What hinders then but we in Heaven may be
Even here on Earth did we but rightly see ?
As mountains, chariots, horsemen all on fire,
To guard Elisha did of old conspire,
Which yet his servant could not see, being blind,
Ourselves environ'd with His joys we find.
Eternity itself is that true light
That doth enclose us being infinite.

The very seas do overflow and swim
With precious nectars as they flow from Him.
The stable Earth which we beneath behold,
Is far more precious than if made of gold.
Fowls, fishes, beasts, trees, herbs, and precious flowers,
Seeds, spices, gums, and aromatic bowers,
Wherewith we are enclos'd and serv'd each day
By His appointment do their tributes pay,
And offer up themselves as gifts of love,
Bestowed on Saints, proceeding from above.
Could we but justly, wisely, truly prize
These blessings, we should be above the skies,
And praises sing with pleasant heart and voice,
Adoring with the Angels should rejoice.
The fertile clouds give rain, the purer air,
Is warm and wholesome, soft and bright and fair.
The stars are wonders which His wisdom names,
The glorious sun the knowing soul enflames.
The very Heavens in their sacred worth,
At once serve us and set His glory forth.
Their influences touch the grateful sense,
They please the eye with their magnificence ;
While in His temple all His saints do sing,
And for His bounty praise their Heavenly King.
All these are in His omnipresence, still
As living waters from His throne they trill ;

As tokens of His love they all flow down
Their beauty, use, and worth the soul do crown.
Men are like Cherubims on either hand
Whose flaming love by His divine command
Is made a sacrifice to ours ; which streams
Throughout all worlds, and fills them all with beams.
We drink our fill, and take their beauty in,
While Jesus' blood refines the soul from sin.
His grievous Cross is a supreme delight,
And of all Heavenly ones the greatest sight.
His Throne is near, 'tis just before our face,
And all Eternity His dwelling-place.
His dwelling-place is full of joys and pleasures,
His throne a fountain of Eternal treasures.
His omnipresence is all sight and love,
Which whoso sees he ever dwells above.
With soft embraces it doth clasp the soul,
And watchfully all enemies control.
It enters in and doth a temple find,
Or make a living one within the mind,
That, while God's omnipresence in us lies,
His treasures might be all before our eyes :
For minds and souls intent upon them here,
Do with the Seraphim's above appear :
And are like spheres of bliss, by love and sight,
By joy, thanksgiving, praise, made infinite.

O give me grace to see Thy face, and be
A constant Mirror of Eternity.
Let my pure soul, transformed to a thought
Attend upon Thy Throne, and, as it ought,
Spend all its time in feeding on Thy love,
And never from Thy sacred presence move.
So shall my conversation ever be
In Heaven, and I, O Lord my God, with Thee !

GOODNESS

I

THE bliss of other men is my delight,
    (When once my principles are right :)
    And every soul which mine doth see
        A treasury.
The face of God is goodness unto all,
And while He thousands to His throne doth call,
    While millions bathe in pleasures,
    And do behold His treasures,
        The joys of all
        On mine do fall,
And even my infinity doth seem
A drop without them of a mean esteem.

II

The light which on ten thousand faces shines,
    The beams which crown ten thousand vines
    With glory, and delight, appear
        As if they were

Reflected only from them all for me,
That I a greater beauty there might see.
Thus stars do beautify
The azure canopy :
Gilded with rays,
Ten thousand ways
They serve me, while the sun that on them shines
Adorns those stars and crowns those bleeding vines.

III

Where goodness is within, the soul doth reign.
Goodness the only Sovereign !
Goodness delights alone to see
Felicity.
And while the Image of His goodness lives
In me, whatever He to any gives
Is my delight and ends
In me, in all my friends :
For goodness is
The spring of bliss,
And 'tis the end of all it gives away
And all it gives it ever doth enjoy.

IV

His goodness ! Lord, it is His highest glory !
The very grace of all His story !

What other thing can me delight
But the blest sight
Of His eternal goodness ? While His love,
His burning love the bliss of all doth prove,
While it beyond the ends
Of Heaven and Earth extends,
And multiplies
Above the skies,
His glory, love, and goodness in my sight
Is for my pleasure made more infinite.

V

The soft and swelling grapes that on their vines
Receive the lively warmth that shines
Upon them, ripen there for me :
Or drink they be,
Or meat. The stars salute my pleased sense
With a derived and borrowed influence :
But better vines do grow,
Far better wines do flow
Above, and while
The Sun doth smile
Upon the lilies there, and all things warm,
Their pleasant odours do my spirit charm.

VI

Their rich affections me like precious seas
   Of nectar and ambrosia please.
   Their eyes are stars, or more divine
     And brighter shine :
Their lips are soft and swelling grapes, their tongues
A quire of blessed and harmonious songs.
   Their bosoms fraught with love
   Are Heavens all Heavens above ;
And being Images of God they are
The highest joys His goodness did prepare.

[THE SOUL'S GLORY]

In making bodies Love could not express
Itself, or art; unless it made them less.
O what a monster had in man been seen,
Had every thumb or toe a mountain been!
What worlds must he devour when he did eat?
What oceans drink?   Yet could not all his meat,
Or stature, make him like an Angel shine;
Or make his soul in glory more divine.
A soul it is that makes us truly great,
Whose little bodies make us more complete.
An Understanding that is Infinite,
An endless, wide, and everlasting sight,
That can enjoy all things and nought exclude,
Is the most sacred greatness may be viewed.
'Twas inconvenient that his bulk should be
An endless hill; he nothing then could see:
No figure have, no motion, beauty, place,
No colour, feature, member, light, or grace:
A body like a mountain is but cumber,
An endless body is but idle lumber.

It spoils converse, and Time itself devours,
While meat in vain in feeding idle powers,
Excessive bulk being most injurious found,
To those conveniences which men have crown'd.
His wisdom did His power here repress,
God made man greater while He made him less.

[FINITE YET INFINITE]

His power bounded, greater is in might,
Than if let loose 'twere wholly infinite.
He could have made an endless Sea by this,
But then it had not been a Sea of Bliss.
Did water from the centre to the skies
Ascend, 'twould drown whatever else we prize.
The Ocean bounded in a finite shore,
Is better far because it is no more,
No use nor glory would in that be seen,
His power made it endless in esteem.
Had not the sun been bounded in its sphere,
Did all the world in one fair flame appear,
And were that flame a real infinite,
'Twould yield no profit, splendour, nor delight.
Its corps confined and beams extended be
Effects of wisdom in the Deity.
One star made infinite would all exclude,
An earth made infinite could ne'er be viewed.
But one being fashioned for the other's sake,
He bounding all, did all most useful make :
And which is best, in profit and delight,
Tho' not in bulk, they all are infinite.

ON NEWS

I

News from a foreign country came,
As if my treasure and my wealth lay there:
So much it did my heart enflame
'Twas wont to call my soul into mine ear,
Which thither went to meet
The approaching sweet,
And on the threshold stood,
To entertain the unknown Good.
It hovered there
As if 'twould leave mine ear,
And was so eager to embrace
The joyful tidings as they came,
'Twould almost leave its dwelling-place,
To entertain that same.

II

As if the tidings were the things,
My very joys themselves, my foreign treasure,
Or else did bear them on their wings;
With so much joy they came, with so much pleasure.

My Soul stood at that gate
   To recreate
Itself with bliss : And to
Be pleased with speed.   A fuller view
   It fain would take,
   Yet journeys back would make
Unto my heart : as if 'twould fain
Go out to meet, yet stay within
To fit a place, to entertain,
   And bring the tidings in.

III

What sacred instinct did inspire
My Soul in childhood with a hope so strong ?
   What secret force mov'd my desire
To expect my joys beyond the seas, so young ?
      Felicity I knew
         Was out of view :
      And being here alone,
   I saw that happiness was gone
         From me ! For this,
      I thirsted absent bliss,
   And thought that sure beyond the seas,
   Or else in something near at hand
   I knew not yet, (since nought did please
      I knew) my Bliss did stand.

IV

But little did the infant dream
That all the treasures of the world were by :
  And that himself was so the cream
And crown of all which round about did lie.
    Yet thus it was : The gem,
      The diadem,
    The ring enclosing all
   That stood upon this earthly ball ;
     The Heavenly Eye,
    Much wider than the sky,
  Wherein they all included were,
  The glorious Soul that was the King
  Made to possess them, did appear
    A small and little thing !

[THE TRIUMPH]

I

A LIFE of Sabbaths here beneath !
Continual Jubilees and Joys !
The days of Heaven, while we breathe
On Earth ! where sin all bliss destroys :
This is a triumph of delights
That doth exceed all appetites !
No joy can be compared to this,
It is a life of perfect bliss.

II

Or perfect bliss !   How can it be ?
To conquer Satan and to reign
In such a vale of misery,
Where vipers, stings and tears remain,
Is to be crowned with victory.
To be content, divine, and free
Even here beneath is great delight,
And next the beatific sight.

III

But inward lusts do oft assail,
Temptations work us much annoy ;
We'll therefore weep, and to prevail
Shall be a more celestial joy.
To have no other enemy
But one ; and to that one to die :
To fight with that and conquer it,
Is better than in peace to sit.

IV

'Tis better for a little time :
For he that all his lusts doth quell,
Shall find this life to be his prime,
And vanquish sin and conquer hell.
The next shall be his double joy,
And that which here seemed to destroy
Shall in the other life appear
A root of Bliss ; a pearl each tear.

[THE ONLY ILL]

I

Sin !
O only fatal woe,
That makes me sad and mourning go !
That all my joys dost spoil,
His Kingdom and my Soul defile !
I never can agree
With Thee.

II

Thou !
Only Thou ! O Thou alone,
And my obdurate Heart of Stone,
The poison and the foes
Or my enjoyments and repose,
The only bitter ill :
Dost kill !

III

Oh!
I cannot meet with thee,
Nor once approach thy memory,
But all my joys are dead,
And all my sacred treasures fled,
As if I now did dwell
In Hell.

IV

Lord!
O hear how short I breathe!
See how I tremble here beneath
A sin! its ugly face
More terror than its dwelling-place
Contains, (O dreadful sin)
Within!

THE RECOVERY

Sin ! wilt thou vanquish me !
And shall I yield the victory ?
    Shall all my joys be spoiled,
        And pleasures soiled
            By thee !
        Shall I remain
        As one that's slain
And never more lift up the head ?
    Is not my Saviour dead !
His blood, thy bane, my balsam, bliss, joy, wine,
Shall thee destroy ; heal, feed, make me divine.

[THE GLORY OF ISRAEL]

I

In Salem dwelt a glorious King,
Rais'd from a shepherd's lowly state,
That did His praises like an angel sing
    Who did the world create.
By many great and bloody wars
He was advanced unto thrones :
But more delighted in the stars
Than in the splendour of his precious stones.
Nor gold nor silver did his eye regard :
The works of God were his sublime reward.

II

A warlike champion he had been,
And many feats of chivalry
Had done : in kingly courts his eye had seen
    A vast variety

Of earthly joys : yet he despised
Those fading honours and false pleasures
Which are by mortals so much prized ;
And placed his happiness in other treasures :
No state of life which in this world we find
Could yield contentment to his greater mind.

III

His fingers touched his trembling lyre,
And every quivering string did yield
A sound that filled all the Jewish quire,
And echoed in the field.
No pleasure was so great to him
As in a silent night to see
The moon and stars : a Cherubim
Above them even here he seemed to be.
Enflamed with love it was his great desire,
To sing, contemplate, ponder, and admire.

IV

He was a prophet and foresaw
Things extant in the world to come :
He was a judge and ruled by a law
That than the honeycomb

Was sweeter far : he was a sage,
And all his people could advise ;
An oracle whose every page
Contained in verse the greatest mysteries :
But most he then enjoy'd himself when he
Did as a poet praise the Deity.

V

A shepherd, soldier, and divine,
A judge, a courtier, and a king,
Priest, angel, prophet, oracle did shine
At once when he did sing.
Philosopher and poet too
Did in his melody appear ;
All these in him did please the view
Of those that did his Heavenly music hear,
And every drop that from his flowing quill
Came down did all the world with nectar fill.

VI

He had a deep and perfect sense
Of all the glories and the pleasures
That in God's works are hid ; the excellence
Of such transcendent treasures

Made him on earth an Heavenly King,
And fill'd his solitudes with joy ;
He never did more sweetly sing
Than when alone, tho' that doth mirth destroy :
Sense did his soul with Heavenly life inspire
And made him seem in God's celestial quire.

VII

Rich, sacred, deep and precious things
Did here on earth the man surround :
With all the glory of the King of Kings
He was most strangely crown'd.
His clear soul and open sight
Among the Sons of God did see
Things filling angels with delight ;
His ear did hear their Heavenly melodie
And when he was alone he all became,
That Bliss implied, or did increase his fame.

VIII

All arts he then did exercise ;
And as his God he did adore,
By secret ravishments above the skies
He carried was before

He died.   His soul did see and feel
What others know not ; and became,
While he before his God did kneel,
A constant Heavenly pure seraphic flame.
O that I might unto his throne aspire,
And all his joys above the stars admire.

ASPIRATION

I

UNTO the spring of purest life
  Aspires my withered heart,
My soul confined in this flesh
  Employs both strength and art
Working, struggling, suing still
  From exile home to part.

II

Who can utter the full joy
  Which that high place doth hold,
Where all the buildings founded are
  On orient pearls untold,
And all the work of those high rooms
  Doth shine with beams of gold !

III

The season is not changed, but still
  Both sun and moon are Bright,
The Lamb of this fair city is
  That clear immortal Light

Whose presence makes eternal day
  Which never ends in night.

IV

Nay all the Saints themselves shall shine
  As bright as brightest sun,
In fullest Triumph crowned they
  To mutual joys shall run,
And safely count their fights and foes
  When once the war is done.

V

For being freed from all defect
  They feel no fleshly war,
Or rather both the flesh and mind
  At length united are,
For joying in so rich a peace
  They can admit no jar.

VI

For ever cheerful and content
  They from mishaps are free ;
No sickness there can threaten health,
  Nor young men old can be :
There they enjoy such happy state
  That in't no change they see.

VII

Who know the Knower of all things
　　What can they choose but know ?
They all behold each other's hearts
　　And all their secrets shew :
One act of will and of not will
　　From all their minds do flow.

VIII

Though all their merits diverse be
　　According to their pains,
Yet Love doth make that every one's
　　Which any other gains,
And all which doth belong to one
　　To all of them pertains.

IX

O Happy Soul which shall behold
　　Thy King still present there,
And mayst from thence behold the world
　　Run round, secure from fear,
With stars and planets, moon and sun,
　　Still moving in their sphere !

X

O King of Kings give me such strength
　In this great War depending,
That I may here prevail at length,
　And ever be ascending,
Till I at last arrive to Thee,
　The Source of all Felicity !

[This poem is not Traherne's, though I have copied it from
his manuscript volume of "Meditations and Devotions." It
is a translation of S. Peter Damiani's hymn, "Ad Perennis
Vitæ Fontem," which has been many times rendered into
English. The above translation is from "The Meditations,
Manuall, and Soliloquia of the Glorious Doctour, St. Augus-
tine," 1631. But it is much abridged and altered in Traherne's
version, and for that reason I have printed it here. Those
who wish to refer to the original version will find it among
the "Inedited Sacred Poems," at the end of Mr. W. T. Brooke's
edition of Giles Fletcher's "Christ's Victory and Triumph."]

[SUPPLICATION]*

I

COME, Holy Ghost, Eternal God,
　　Our hearts with Life inspire,
Enkindle zeal in all our Souls,
　　And fill us with Thy Heavenly fire.

II

Send forth Thy Beams and let Thy Grace
　　Upon my spirit shine,
That I may all Thy works enjoy,
　　Revive, sing praises, be Divine.

* It is doubtful whether this poem is by Traherne.

AN HYMN UPON
ST. BARTHOLOMEW'S DAY

I

WHAT powerful Spirit lives within !
What active Angel doth inhabit here !
　What heavenly light inspires my skin,
Which doth so like a Deity appear !
A Living Temple of all ages, I
　　Within me see
　A Temple of Eternity !
　　All Kingdoms I descry
　　In me.

II

An inward Omnipresence here
Mysteriously like His within me stands
　Whose knowledge is a Sacred Sphere
That in itself at once includes all lands.

There is some Angel that within me can
　　Both talk and move,
　And walk and fly and see and love,
　　A man on earth, a man
　　　Above.

III

　Dull walls of clay my Spirit leaves,
And in a foreign Kingdom doth appear,
　This great Apostle it receives
Admires His works and sees them, standing here.
Within myself from East to West I move
　　As if I were
　At once a Cherubim and Sphere,
　　Or was at once above
　　　And here.

IV

　The Soul's a messenger whereby
Within our inward Temple we may be
　Even like the very Deity
In all the parts of His Eternity.
O live within and leave unweildy dross !
　　Flesh is but clay !
　O fly my Soul and haste away
　　To Jesus' Throne or Cross—
　　　Obey !

POEMS EXTRACTED FROM TRAHERNE'S "CHRISTIAN ETHICKS"

[ALL the following poems (excepting those in the "Appendix") are taken from Traherne's "Christian Ethicks." That they are all from his own pen cannot, I think, be doubted. They are entirely in his manner, and have little or no resemblance to that of any other poet. As the reader will see, I have, where necessary, quoted a few sentences from Traherne's prose in order to render the design of the verses more intelligible.]

[From pp. 344-5]

How glorious the Counsel and Design of God is for the Atchieving of this Great End, for the making of all Vertues more compleat and Excellent, and for the Heightening of their Beauty and Perfection we will exemplifie here in the Perfection of Courage. For the Height and depth and Splendor of every Vertue is of great Concernment to the Perfection of the Soul since the Glory of its Life is seated in

the Accomplishment of its essence, in the fruit it yieldeth in
its Operations.   Take it in Verse made long ago upon this
occasion—

> For Man to Act as if his Soul did see
> The very Brightness of Eternity ;
> For Man to Act as if his Love did burn
> Above the Spheres, even while it's in its Urne ;
> For Man to Act even in the Wilderness,
> As if he did those Sovereign Joys possess,
> Which do at once confirm, stir up, enflame,
> And perfect Angels ; having not the same !
> It doth increase the value of his Deeds,
> In this a Man a Seraphim exceeds.
> To Act on Obligations yet unknown,
> To Act upon Rewards as yet unshewn,
> To keep Commands whose Beauty's yet unseen,
> To Cherish and retain a Zeal between
> Sleeping and waking ; shews a constant care,
> And that a deeper Love, a Love so rare,
> That no Eye Service may with it compare.
> The Angels, who are faithful while they view
> His Glory, know not what themselves would do,
> Were they in our Estate !   A Dimmer Light
> Perhaps would make them erre as well as We
> And in the Coldness of a darker Night
> Forgetful and Lukewarm Themselves might be.

Our very Rust shall cover us with Gold,
Our Dust shall sprinkle* while their Eyes behold
The Glory Springing from a feeble State,
Where meer Belief doth, if not conquer Fate
Surmount and pass what it doth Antedate.

[From p. 326]

In Matters of Art the force of Temperance is undeniable.
It relateth not only to our Meats and Drinks, but to all our
Behaviours, Passions, and Desires.

All Musick, Sawces, Feasts, Delights and Pleasures,
Games, Dancing, Arts consist in govern'd Measures;
Much more do Words and Passions of the Mind
In Temperance their sacred Beauty find.

[From pp. 347-9]

If you say it would be Beneficial to God or to that Spectator
or that intelligible Power, that Spirit for whom it was made :
It is apparent that no Corporeal Being can be serviceable to a
Spirit but only by the Beauty of those Services it performeth
to other Corporeals that are capable of receiving them, and
that therefore all Corporeals must be limited and bounded for
each other's sake. And for this Cause it is that a Philosophical
Poet said :

As in a Clock, 'tis hinder'd Force doth bring
The Wheels to order'd Motion by a Spring ;

* (?) Sparkle.

Which order'd Motion guides a steddy Hand
In useful sort at Figures just to stand ;
Which, were it not by Counter-ballance staid,
The Fabrick quickly would aside be laid
As wholly useless : So a Might too Great
But well proportion'd makes the World compleat.
Power well-bounded is more Great in Might
Than if let loose 'twere wholly Infinite.
He could have made an endless Sea by this,
But then it had not been a Sea of Bliss ;
A Sea that's bounded in a finite shore
Is better far because it is no more.
Should Waters endlessly exceed the Skies
They'd drown the World, and all whate'er we prize.
Had the bright Sun been Infinite its Flame
Had burnt the World, and quite consumed the same.
That Flame would yield no splendour to the Sight,
'Twould be but Darkness though 'twere Infinite.
One Star made Infinite would all exclude,
An Earth made Infinite could ne'er be view'd.
But all being bounded for each other's sake,
He, bounding all, did all most useful make ;
And which is best, in Profit and Delight
Though not in Bulk, he made all Infinite !
He, in his Wisdom, did their use extend
By all, to all the World from End to End.

In all Things all Things service do to all ;
And thus a Sand is Endless, though most small,
  And every Thing is truly Infinite
  In its Relation deep and exquisite.

[From p. 383 in Chapter XXV On Meekness]

  Were all the World a Paradise of Ease
      'Twere easie then to live in Peace.
  Were all men Wise, Divine, and Innocent,
    Just, Holy, Peaceful and Content,
    Kind, Loving, True and alwaies Good
    As in the Golden-Age they stood ;
      'Twere easie then to live
    In all Delight and Glory, full of Love,
    Blest as the Angels are above.

  But we such Principles must now attain
      (If we true blessedness would gain)
  As those are which will help to make us reign
    Over Disorders, Injuries,
    Ingratitudes, Calamities,
    Affronts, Oppressions, Slanders, Wrongs,
      Lies, Angers, bitter Tongues ;
    The reach of Malice must surmount, and quell
    The very Rage and Power of Hell.

[From pp. 394-9]

OF MEEKNESS

I

MANKIND is sick, the World distemper'd lies
    Opprest with Sins and Miseries.
Their Sins are Woes; a long corrupted Train
    Of Poyson, drawn from Adam's vein,
Stains all his seed, and all his Kin
    Are one Disease of Life within;
       They all torment themselves!
The World's one Bedlam, or a greater Cave
    Of Mad-men that do alwaies rave.

II

The Wise and Good like kind Physicians are,
    That strive to heal them by their Care;
They Physick and their Learning calmly use
    Although the Patient them abuse,
For since the Sickness is (they find)
A sad Distemper of the Mind,
       All railings they impute,
All Injuries, unto the sore Disease
    They are expresly come to ease.

III

If we would to the World's distempered Mind
  Impute the Rage which there we find,
We might, even in the midst of all our Foes
    Enjoy and feel a sweet Repose,
    Might pity all the Griefs we see,
    Anointing every Malady
    With precious Oil and Balm;
And while ourselves are calm, our Art improve
  To rescue them and show our Love.

IV

But let's not fondly our own selves beguile ;
  If we Revile 'cause they Revile,
Ourselves infected with their sore Disease
    Need other's Helps to give us ease ;
For we more Mad than they remain,
    Need to be cut, and need a Chain
    Far more than they.   Our Brain
    Is craz'd, and if we put our Wit to theirs,
    We may be justly made their Heirs.

V

But while with open eyes we clearly see
  The brightness of His Majesty ;

While all the World by Sin to Satan sold,
   In daily Wickedness grows old,
   Men in chains of Darkness lye,
   In Bondage and Iniquity,
      And pierce and grieve themselves!
The dismal Woes wherein they crawl, enhance
   The peace of our Inheritance.

VI

We wonder to behold our selves so nigh
   To so much Sin and Misery,
And yet to see our selves so safe from harm!
   What Amulet, what hidden Charm
     Could fortifie and raise the Soul
   So far above them and controul
     Such fierce Malignity?
The brightness and the glory which we see
   Is made a greater Mystery.

VII

And while we feel how much our God doth love
   The Peace of Sinners, how much move
And sue, and thirst, intreat, lament, and grieve
   For all the Crimes in which they live,

And seek and wait and call again,
And long to save them from the pain
  Of Sin, from all their Woe !
With greater thirst as well as grief we try,
  How to relieve their Misery.

VIII

The life and splendour of Felicity,
  Whose floods so overflowing be,
The streams of Joy which round about his Throne
  Enrich and fill each Holy One,
  Are so abundant, that we can
  Spare all, even all to any Man !
    And have it all ourselves !
Nay, have the more !   We long to make them see
    The sweetness of Felicity.

IX

While we contemplate their Distresses, how
  Blind Wretches, they in bondage bow,
And tear and wound themselves, and vex and groan,
  And chafe and fret so near His Throne
  And know not what they ail, but lye
    Tormented in their Misery,
    (Like Mad-men that are blind)

In works of darkness nigh such full Delight :
    That they might find and see the sight,

X

What would we give ! that these might likewise see
    The Glory of His Majesty
The joy and fulness of that high delight
    Whose Blessedness is infinite !
  We would even cease to live, to gain
  Them from their misery and pain,
    And make them with us reign,
For they themselves would be our greatest Treasures,
    When sav'd our own most Heavenly Pleasures.

XI

O holy Jesus who didst for us die,
    And on the Altar bleeding lie,
Bearing all torment, pain, reproach, and shame,
    That we, by vertue of the same,
    Though enemies to God, might be
    Redeem'd and set at liberty :
      As thou didst us forgive,
So meekly let us love to others shew,
    And live in Heaven on Earth below.

XII

Let's prize their Souls, and let them be our Gems,
  Our Temples and our Diadems,
Our Brides, our Friends, our fellow-Members, Eyes,
  Hands, Hearts and Souls, our Victories,
  And Spoils and Trophies, our own Joys !
  Compar'd to Souls all else are Toys ;
    O Jesus, let them be
  Such unto us as they are unto Thee,
    Vessels of Glory and Felicity !

XIII

How will they love us, when they find our Care
Brought them all thither where they are !
When they conceive what terror 'tis to dwell
  In all the punishments of Hell ;
  And in a lively manner see,
  O Christ, eternal Joys in thee !
    How will they all delight
In praising Thee for us with all their might !
  How sweet a Grace, how infinite !

[From p. 425]

OF CONTENTMENT

CONTENTMENT is a sleepy thing
  If it in Death alone must die ;
A quiet Mind is worse than Poverty,
  Unless it from Enjoyment spring !
That's Blessedness alone that makes a King !
Wherein the Joys and Treasures are so great,
They all the powers of the Soul employ,
      And fill it with a Work compleat,
      While it doth all enjoy.
True Joys alone Contentment do inspire,
Enrich Content and make our Courage higher.
      Content alone's a dead and silent Stone ;
        The real life of Bliss
      Is Glory reigning in a Throne,
        Where all Enjoyment is.
      The Soul of Man is so inclin'd to see,
      Without his Treasures no man's Soul can be,
        Nor rest content Uncrown'd !
        Desire and Love
Must in the height of all their Rapture move,
        Where there is true Felicity.
Employment is the very life and ground

Of Life itself ; whose pleasant Motion is
      The form of Bliss :
All Blessedness a life with Glory Crown'd :
Life ! Life is all ; in its most full extent
Stretcht out to all things, and with all Content !

[From p. 456, Of Magnanimity]

And if the Glory and Esteem I have,
Be nothing else than what my Silver gave,
      If, for no other ground,
I am with Love or Praises crown'd,
'Tis such a shame, such vile, such base Repute,
'Tis better starve than eat such empty Fruit.

APPENDIX

THE poems in the foregoing pages are derived (as I have already explained) from three separate MS. volumes, and from the author's prose volume, entitled "Christian Ethicks." The bulk of them (ending with "Goodness") are from the folio volume. The remainder—with the exception of the three which are from the volume of "Meditations and Devotions"—are from the prose volume entitled "Centuries of Meditations." I have printed all the poems which I have found in these various sources, with one exception. This is a poem which appears in the folio volume, but which is there crossed through as though marked for suppression.* Whether this mark of suppression was made by the author or by another person there are no means of judging; but as the poem in question

* Several passages in other poems are thus marked. Usually where these marks appear—but not invariably so—there is a slight falling off in the author's inspiration. As these passages, however, could not be omitted without leaving palpable *lacunæ* in the poems, I have taken no notice of them (save in one instance where I have suppressed a stanza which is clearly superfluous), preferring to leave the critical reader to discover such inequalities for himself.

is, as I think, somewhat below the level of its companions,
I have thought it better to reserve it for the appendix than
to print it between the poems " Thoughts " I. and II.,
where it occurs in the MS.

BLISS

I

ALL Bliss
Consists in this,
To do as Adam did,
And not to know those superficial Toys
Which in the Garden once were hid.
Those little new-invented things,
Cups, saddles, crowns are childish joys,
So ribbands are and rings,
Which all our happiness destroys.

II

Nor God
In His abode,
Nor Saints, nor little boys,
Nor Angels made them ; only foolish men,
Grown mad with custom, on those toys,

Which more increase their wants, do dote,
And when they older are do then
  Those baubles chiefly note
With greedier eyes, more boys tho' men.

To enable the reader to judge whether my hypothesis
that the author of " A Serious and Patheticall Contempla-
tion of the Mercies of God " is also the author of the
other poems contained in the present volume, is well or ill-
founded, I will now print the three poems which appear
in the above-mentioned work.   They are as follows :

[LIFE'S BLESSEDNESS]

WHILE I, O Lord, exalted by Thy hand
Above the skies, in glory seem to stand,
The skies being made to serve me, as they do,
While I thy Glories in thy Goodness view.
To be in Glory higher than the skies
Is greater bliss than 'tis in place to rise
Above the Stars : More blessed and divine
To live and see than like the Sun to shine.
O what Profoundness in my Body lies
For whom the Earth was made, the Sea, the Skies !
So greatly high our human Bodies are
That Angels scarcely may with these compare :

In all the heights of Glory seated, they
Above the Sun in Thine eternal day
Are seen to shine ; with greater gifts adorned
Than Gold with Light or Flesh with Life suborned ;
Suns are but Servants, Skies beneath their feet ;
The Stars but Stones ; Moons but to serve them meet.
Beyond all heights above the World they reign
In thy great Throne ordained to remain.
All Tropes are Clouds ; Truth doth itself excel,
Whatever Heights Hyperboles can tell.

[THE RESURRECTION]

THEN shall each Limb a spring of Joy be found,
And every member with its Glory crown'd :
While all the Senses, fill'd with all the Good
That ever Ages in them understood
Transported are : Containing Worlds of Treasure
At one delight with all their Joy and Pleasure,
From whence, like Rivers, Joy shall ever flow,
Affect the Soul, though in the Body grow,
Return again and make the Body shine
Like Jesus Christ, while both in one combine.
Mysterious Contracts are between the Soul,
Which touch the Spirits and by those its Bowl ;

The Marrow, Bowels, Spirits, melt and move,
Dissolving ravish, teach them how to love.
He that could bring the Heavens thro' the eye,
And make the World within the Fancy lie,
By beams of Light that closing meet in one,
From all the parts of His celestial Throne,
Far more than this in framing Bliss can do,
Inflame the Body and the Spirit too :
Can make the Soul by Sense to feel and see,
And with her Joy the Senses wrap'd to be :
Yea, while the Flesh or Body subject lies
To those Affections which in Souls arise ;
All holy Glories from the Soul redound,
And in the Body by the Soul abound,
Are felt within and ravish ev'ry Sense
With all the Godhead's glorious Excellence,
Who found the way Himself to dwell within,
As if even Flesh were nigh to Him of kin :
His Goodness, Wisdom, Power, Love Divine,
Make by the Soul convey'd the Body shine,
Not like the Sun (that earthly Darkness is)
But in the strengths and heights of all this bliss,
For God designed thy Body for His sake,
A Temple of the Deity to make.

THE WAYS OF WISDOM

"Her ways are ways of pleasantness, and all
her paths are peace."

THESE sweeter far than lilies are,
No roses may with these compare !
    How these excel
    No tongue can tell,
Which he that well and truly knows
    With praise and joy he goes !
How great and happy's he that knows his ways
    To be divine and heavenly Joys :
To whom each city is more brave
Than walls of pearl and streets which gold doth pave :
    Whose open eyes
    Behold the skies ;
Who loves their wealth and beauty more
    Than kings love golden ore !
Who sees the heavenly ancient ways
Of God the Lord with joy and praise,
    More than the skies
    With open eyes
Doth prize them all ; yea, more than gems,
    And regal diadems ;
That more esteemeth mountains, as they are,
    Than if they gold and silver were :

To whom the sun more pleasure brings
Than crowns and thrones and palaces to kings :
    That knows his ways
    To be the joys
And way of God—those things who knows
    With joy and praise he goes !

I do not think it is necessary to spend much time or ink in endeavouring to prove that the author of these three poems must have been also the writer of the other poems contained in this volume. Unless it be contended that no conclusion as to authorship can be drawn from similarity of style, sentiment, and peculiarities of expression, I do not see how it is possible for any one who carefully considers the matter to entertain a reasonable doubt about it. Not even the hypothesis of imitation by one author of the style of another can here be entertained—for no man can imitate what is not known to him.

Every poet has his special topics, his favourite terms of expression, his peculiar vocabulary, and even his pet rhymes, which are bound to appear often in his verse. I think it may be truly said that there is nothing in the three poems taken from " A Serious and Patheticall Contemplation of the Mercies of God " which cannot be paralleled in the other poems contained in this volume. All are characterised by the same fervent piety, the same command of expression and musical diction, the same dwelling upon the ideas that though God is necessary to man, yet man also is necessary to God, and that the body (instead of being, according to the ordinary theological belief, a *corpus vile* of corruption) is " a spring of Joy " crowned with glory ; and the same continual allusions to the great natural phenomena.   When to these resemblances we add the many small coincidences of words and phrases which are always recurring in the poems, the evidence of common authorship becomes too strong to be resisted.

Perhaps it may be worth while to quote a few instances of these resemblances out of the many which might be given.   In the second stanza of " The Person " we have

> Men's hands than angels' wings
> Are truer wealth even here below.

In " Life's Blessedness " we have

> So greatly high our human bodies are
> That Angels scarcely may with them compare.

In the fifth stanza of " The Estate " we have

> The laws of God, the Works he did create,
> His ancient ways, are His and my Estate.

In " The Ways of Wisdom " we have

> Who sees the heavenly ancient ways.

In " Thoughts IV." we have

> The very heavens in their sacred worth
> At once serve us and set his Glory forth.

In " Life's Blessedness " we have

> The skies being made to serve me, as they do,
> While I Thy Glories in Thy Goodness view.

In " The Influx " we have

> No soul but stone, no man but clay am I.

In " Life's Blessedness " we have

> The stars but stones.

The reader will doubtless have observed that our poet was very fond of using " treasure " and " pleasure " as rhymes. He seldom omits to bring them in in a poem of any length, and it will be observed that they are introduced in " The Resurrection." Certain defective rhymes (or no rhymes) also occur pretty frequently, as " lay," " joy," " away," " enjoy." In " The Ways of Wisdom " we have " ways " and " joys."

I think I have produced evidence enough to convince the reader of the soundness of my contention : if not, I will undertake to produce a good deal more. It is fortunate, indeed, that " A Serious and Patheticall Contemplation " should have stolen into print (for neither at the time of its publication nor subsequently does it appear to have attracted any attention), since without it we should have had no clue to the authorship of these poems.

Mr. W. T. Brooke has discovered in the British Museum a broadside with the following title, "A Congratulatory Poem on the Right Honourable Sr Orlando Bridgman, Lord Keeper of the Great Seal of England," which, he suggests, may possibly have been written by the author of the poems here printed. But though it is a poem of considerable merit, it has, in my opinion, no correspondence in style with Traherne's poems. A few lines from it, however, will not be altogether out of place here :

Were all your own Rolls searcht scarce should we find
That noble seat filled with so fit a mind :
So brave a mind as baseness ne'er allays,
So great a mind as greatness cannot raise,
So just a mind as interest can't seduce,
So wise a mind as colours can't abuse,
So large a mind as largest Trusts do crave,
So calm a mind as Equity should have.
High Courtships construed in the present tense,
Law's Oracle without perplexed sense,
A sober piety in a virtuoso,
And an Orlando without Furioso.

TRAHERNE'S "SERIOUS AND PATHETICALL CONTEMPLATION OF THE MERCIES OF GOD"

THIS book would hardly be complete without some account of the above work. It is a small 12mo volume of 146 pages, with an engraved frontispiece. It is written —excepting the three pieces of verse which I have already printed—in a kind of unrhymed verse, which is curiously suggestive of the style of Whitman's "Leaves of Grass," particularly in the frequent passages in which the author enumerates or catalogues, as the American poet does, every object he can think of which bears any relation to his theme. There were, of course, more points of unlikeness than of likeness between the two poets, but they at least resembled each other in their invincible optimism, as well as in the points mentioned above. Whitman could not have known of the existence of the "Serious and Patheticall Contemplation"; but had it been accessible to him, it might well have been suspected that he was under some obligations to it.

The booklet consists of a series of "Thanksgivings" for the Body, the Soul, the Glory of God's Works, the Blessedness of God's Ways, the Wisdom of His Word, &c. There is much poetry and beauty of expression in these

"Thanksgivings," and they are valuable also for the light which they occasionally throw upon passages in the poems which might else seem obscure. Thus the following passages from the "Thanksgiving for the Body" may be profitably compared with "The Salutation" and "Wonder":

I will praise Thee, for I am fearfully and wonderfully made, marvellous are Thy works; and that my Soul knoweth right well.

My substance was not hid from Thee when I was made in secret and curiously wrought in the lowest parts of the earth.

Thine eyes did see my substance yet being unperfect; and in thy book all my members were written; which in continuance were fashioned when as yet there was none of them.

*   *   *   *   *

O Lord!
Thou hast given me a body,
Wherein the glory of Thy Power shineth,
Wonderfully composed above the beasts,
Within distinguished into useful parts,
Beautified without with many ornaments.
Limbs rarely pois'd,
And made for Heaven:
Arteries fill'd
With celestial spirits:
Veins wherein blood floweth,

Refreshing all my flesh.
  Like rivers :
Sinews fraught with the mystery
  Of wonderful strength,
    Stability,
    Feeling.
O blessed be Thy glorious Name !
  That Thou hast made it
    A Treasury of Wonders,
  Fit for its several Ages ;
    For Dissections,
    For Sculptures in Brass,
    For Draughts in Anatomy,
  For the contemplation of the Sages.

I quote the following passage from " A Thanksgiving and Prayer for the Nation " not merely because it is fine in itself, but also because it affords us yet another interesting glimpse of the author's personality :

O Lord, the children of my people are Thy peculiar treasures,
Make them mine, O God, even while I have them,
My lovely companions, like Eve in Eden !
So much my treasure that all other wealth is without them
    But dross and poverty.
Do they not adorn and beautifie the World,
  And gratify my Soul which hateth Solitude !
Thou, Lord, hast made thy servant a sociable creature, for
  which I praise thy name,

A lover of company, a delighter in equals ;
  Replenish the inclination which Thyself hath implanted,
And give me eyes
To see the beauty of that life and comfort
Wherewith those by their actions
      Inspire the nations.
Their Markets, Tillage, Courts of Judicature, Marriages, Feasts
    and Assemblies, Navys, Armies,
Priests and Sabbaths, Trades and Business, the voice of the
    Bridegroom, Musical Instruments, the light of Candles,
    and the grinding of Mills
Are comfortable, O Lord, let them not cease.
The riches of the land are all the materials of my felicity in
    their hands :
They are my Factors, Substitutes, and Stewards ;
Second Selves, who by Trade and Business animate my wealth,
Which else would be dead and rust in my hands ;
But when I consider, O Lord, how they come unto thy
    Temples, fill thy Courts, and sing Thy praises,
  O how wonderful they then appear !
        What Stars,
        Enflaming Suns,
        Enlarging Seas
          Of Divine Affection,
        Confirming Paterns,
        Infusing Influence,
          Do I feel in these !
        Who are the shining light
        Of all the land (to my very Soul :)

Wings and Streams
Carrying me unto thee,
The Sea of Goodness from whence they came.

Have we not here a very remarkable anticipation of the
leading thought of Whitman's "Leaves of Grass"? Do
we not see in both poets the same deep love of and delight
in humanity, the same feeling of comradeship and brother-
hood with all men, the same hunger for sympathy and
reciprocal affection, the same pleasure in the common
things of life and nature, and the same frank acceptance
of things as they are, and not as they might be? I have
said that there is more unlikeness than likeness between
the poets—but is it really so? Does not the above passage
show that beneath all apparent differences there was a
fundamental resemblance in their characters? To say the
least, there was this resemblance—that both of them found
life supremely well worth living, and never doubted, even
when the clouds were blackest, that the sun was shining
beyond them.

THE WILL OF THOMAS TRAHERNE, AS REGISTERED IN THE PREROGATIVE COURT OF CANTERBURY

MEMORANDUM that Thomas Traherne late of Teddington in the County of Midd Clerk deceased in the time of the sickness whereof he dyed and vpon or about the Seaven and Twentyth of September 1674 having sent for John Berdo Gent to come to him the said Thomas Traherne then lying sick at the Lady Bridgmans house in Teddington and the said Mr Berdo being come vnto him he the said Thomas Traherne being then of perfect mind and memory vsed these or the like words to the said Mr. Berdo viz! I haue sent for you to make my Will for mee or to that effect Whereupon the said Mr Berdo asked of him the said Mr Thomas Traherne whether he would haue it made in Writing To which the said Thomas Traherne answeared in these or the like words viz! Noe I haue not so much but that I can dispose of it by Word of Mouth or to that effect And the said Thomas Traherne being then of perfect mind and memory by Word of Mouth with an intent to make his Will and to settle and dispose of his Goods and Estate did vtter and speake these or the like words viz! I desire my Lady Bridgman and her daughter the Lady Charlott should haue each of them a Ring And to you (speaking to the said Mr. Berdo) I give Tenn Pounds and to Mrs Cockson Tenn shillings and to Phillipp Landman ffyve shillings and to John Rowland the Gardiner ffyve shillings and to Mary the Laundry maid ffyve shillings and to all the rest of the servants half a crowne apeece. My best Hatt I give it to my brother Phillipp And sister (speaking to Mrs Susan Traherne the wife of his brother Phillipp which Susan was then present) I desire you would keepe it for him And all the rest of my Clothes that is worth your acceptance I give to you And for those that are not worth your accepting I would have you to giue them to Phillipp Landman or to whome you please with my old Hatt All my Books I give to my brother Phillipp And (still speaking to the said Mrs Susan then present) I make you and my brother Phillipp my whole Executors which words or the like in effect The said Thomas Traherne being then of perfect mind and memory did then utter Animo testandi and with an intent that the same should stand and be as and for his last Will and Testament in the presence and hearing of John Berdo Alice Cockson and Mary Linum.

John Berdo Alice Cockson The Mark of Mary Linum.

Proved at London 22 Oct 1674 by Susan Traherne, one of the Executors, to whom administration was granted, power being reserved of making the like grant to Philip Traherne, the other executor, should he ask for the same.